Stop *Effing  Yourself

SEAN KENNIFF, M.D.

D1211234

Health Communications, Inc.
Deerfield Beach, Florida

www.hcibooks.com

Library of Congress Cataloging-in-Publication Data

Kenniff, Sean.
  Stop *effing yourself : a survivor's guide to life's biggest screw-ups /
Sean Kenniff.
    p. cm.
  Includes bibliographical references and index.
  ISBN-13: 978-0-7573-1469-8
  ISBN-10: 0-7573-1469-4
  1. Self-defeating behavior.   2. Failure (Psychology)   3. Success—Psychological
aspects.   I. Title.
  BF637.S8K42 2010
  158.1—dc22

                                                                  2010008464

©2010 Sean Kenniff

HCI, its logos, and marks are trademarks of Health Communications, Inc.

Publisher: Health Communications, Inc.
        3201 S.W. 15th Street
        Deerfield Beach, FL 33442–8190

Cover and interior designs by Lawna Patterson Oldfield

Contents

*eff (ef') *n.* An act of self-sabotage.—*v.* To sabotage one's own efforts. ***eff•ed**.

*eff•ing (ef'ing) *v.i.* To be in the act of self-sabotage.

—*adj.* Of or pertaining to an act of self-sabotage.

*eff•er (ef'r) *n.* A person who repeatedly engages in self-sabotage.

Introduction

Nobody knew it, but I had a huge *effing problem . . .

That's not easy to admit, because to the outside observer, my life looks pretty remarkable. I'm a doctor—a neurologist—and a good one. I'm fit and thankfully healthy. I earn a handsome salary. I starred on the nation's number one television show—the first season of *Survivor*—and I have made guest appearances on many other popular programs. I've met scores of celebrities, movers, and shakers. I've appeared in a movie and acted in a soap opera. Millions of Americans watched me each week as I reported important health news on a major television network, and I had my own health advice column in a prominent U.S. daily newspaper. I have my own radio show. I've dated kind, spectacular, and brilliant women. I have a wonderful family, devoted friends, and few—if any—enemies. And along the way I've managed to change several lives—and I've saved a few too. Sounds pretty good, right?

I hid my secret well.

On the inside things were very different. I had no idea how much money I had in the bank. I had no growing investments. I didn't own my car or my home. I had little savings. I owed the IRS some money—okay, make that *a lot* of money. My romantic life was in shambles, and like many men I had no clue what I was doing wrong. I had stopped exercising. I was gaining weight. I spent too much time drinking beer with my buddies. My body was hurting in weird places. I wasn't sleeping well. I was unhappy and stressed a lot of the time. I felt like a fraud—a house of cards teetering on collapse. Every day I lived in fear that my inadequacies would be discovered. Sooner or later someone would see my string, start pulling, and I'd unravel like a spool of yarn. I was paralyzed by uncertainty and insecurity. In a nutshell, I felt miserable about myself. So I did what anybody would do—I watched a lot of *Oprah*. But my problem was way beyond Oprah's powerful pick-me-ups; it was even beyond the tough talk of Dr. Phil. I was a world-class self-saboteur, and I was royally *effed.

This was self-sabotage. These messes were mine.

True *Effing Story

Leading up to the turn of the millennium, I skipped out on some of my student loan payments because I thought the Y2K computer glitch might wipe away my educational debt.

I don't know what triggered that revelation, but one day, after years of ignorance, it happened. I decided to take a personal inventory. It was an honest and unpleasant analysis of who I was, what I wanted to be, and what I had become. From my early twenties to my early thirties, I had accomplished a lot but had grown very little. My impulsive inner child was not only running my life but ruining it. Some people, as Pablo Picasso famously did, can harness that inner child to create breathtaking bursts of artistry. But my inner child was, in fact, a problem child—and it was turning me into a problem adult.

> My inner child was a problem child—and it was turning me into a problem adult.

For years *I chose* to spend out of control, and *I failed* to save money or invest it wisely. *I chose* to work long hours. *I chose* to put limits and strains on romantic relationships. *I failed* to nurture important friendships. *I failed* to prioritize a healthy diet and exercise plan. *I chose* stress over simplicity. *I chose* haplessness and helplessness over happiness. And time after time when I was given opportunities to improve my situation, I either *failed* to act, or *I chose* actions that would make it harder for me to achieve my goals. From the moment I had my revelation, it was clear: if I wanted to start living my dreams, I had to first stop living my delusions.

And I needed to stop immediately.

There are many fascinating psychological theories on why people sabotage their own efforts. For me it's a combination of things: fear of success, fear of failure, insecurity, some guilty feelings, and a dash of complacency. After reviewing the available science and analyzing countless acts of self-sabotage in my own life, I am now convinced that we all have an inner voice that is discouraging, distracting, demanding, and damaging. Some experts call this voice the "internal enemy," and by listening to this internal enemy, we engage in self-defeating behaviors. I was surprised to learn that self-sabotage provides some emotional and psychological comforts; for one, it allows us to stay the same. Emotional growth requires change, and it is always uncomfortable, and self-sabotage may be some sort of ego-preserving psychological default setting. But you don't have to listen to that internal enemy, and you can even change your internal enemy into an ally if you know how to do it. And that's what *Stop *Effing Yourself* is about.

If my story sounds familiar to you, then this book is going to be tremendously helpful. For my own personal struggle with self-sabotage, I scoured the scientific literature and enlisted the help of renowned experts in health, personal finance, career building, relationships, and romance. The valuable insight and guidance I received is provided in the following chapters. Unlike other books written on self-sabotage, *Stop *Effing Yourself* will help you recognize the patterns in your own life, identify the ten biggest *effing problems you might be making in key life areas, and provide you with ten explicit *effing solutions. *Stop *Effing Yourself* is not just a self-help book—it is a how-to manual.

Now let me ask you something . . .

*Do You Have an *Effing Problem?*

To *eff is human. We all self-sabotage from time to time, but some people do it more frequently and with more gusto than others. Self-sabotage guarantees failure. That does not mean that people who sabotage themselves are failures; in fact, quite the opposite is true. Many people with big *effing problems are driven, intelligent, artistic, and thoughtful people, but they just never complete those critical final steps to lifelong success.

Acts of self-sabotage always prevent you from living up to your fullest potential, achieving your goals, or manifesting your dreams. And like a disease, self-sabotage spreads quickly, moving from one area of your life to the next. Sabotaging your finances has an immediate impact on your career and family life. Sabotaging your marriage strains relationships with children and other family members, but it can also have an immediate impact on your bank account—just ask any divorcé. For some, self-sabotage becomes a way of life. Their plans never seem to work out because they are subconsciously working against themselves. So how big are your *effing problems? Grab a pencil and take the quiz on the following pages.

Do You Have an *Effing Problem?

1. Have you gained more than 20 lbs. since high school?   ○ Yes ○ No

2. Have you tried several times to lose weight and failed?   ○ Yes ○ No

3. Have you developed any chronic medical conditions?   ○ Yes ○ No

4. Are you uncomfortable naked?   ○ Yes ○ No

5. Do you smoke cigarettes, do drugs, or drink in excess?   ○ Yes ○ No

6. Have you ever done something you should have been arrested for?   ○ Yes ○ No

7. Have you ever driven under the influence of drugs or alcohol?   ○ Yes ○ No

8. Has your sexual behavior been risky at times?   ○ Yes ○ No

9. Have you ever had a sexually transmitted disease (STD)?   ○ Yes ○ No

10. Have you repeated the same mistakes in different romantic relationships?   ○ Yes ○ No

11. Have you had an argument with anyone this week?   ○ Yes ○ No

12. Do you wish you could undo your current romantic relationship?   ○ Yes ○ No

13. Are you in love with someone else?   ○ Yes ○ No

14. Have you ever cheated on a spouse or significant other?   ○ Yes ○ No

15. Have you changed jobs more than two times in the last five years?   ○ Yes ○ No

16. Are your coworkers hard to get along with?   ○ Yes ○ No

17. Are you insecure about your finances?   ○ Yes ○ No

18. Do you rent your home?   ○ Yes ○ No

19. Do you lose track of your money?   ○ Yes ○ No

20. Do you avoid paying bills?   ○ Yes ○ No

21. Are you having serious family issues? (kids or others)   ○ Yes ○ No

22. Do you feel like a fraud sometimes?   ○ Yes ○ No

23. Do you procrastinate?   ○ Yes ○ No

24. Are you a perfectionist?   ○ Yes ○ No

25. Do you complain a lot?   ○ Yes ○ No

Give yourself one point for each "Yes" answer and
add up your score. How did you do?

Score   Size of Your *Effing Problem

1–5 .... **Not** *Effing Bad

6–10 .... **Normal** *Effing Problems

11–15 .... **Bad** *Effing Problems

16–20 .... **Very Bad** *Effing Problems

20–25 .... **Serious** *Effing Problems—Help Needed!

When I first took the quiz, I scored a 19. That was Very Bad *Effing Problems, but today I score a solid 6. That's progress! You can make that type of progress too with the help of this book. There are five chapters in *Stop *Effing Yourself,* and they cover a wide range of self-defeating behaviors. I recommend reading all of them. However, if you really want to stop *effing yourself, it is important to start with the biggest *effing problem in your life—for most people, it's poor health.

1 Your *Effing Unhealthy Lifestyle

THE #1 *EFFING PROBLEM: YOU'RE A DIET ADDICT

Take a look around—almost everyone is fatter than they should be. Our waistlines have steadily ballooned over the last three decades before finally leveling off in the past few years. Obesity has been declared public enemy number one by both the Centers for Disease Control (CDC) and the American Medical Association (AMA). Obesity is the second leading cause of preventable death in the United States, and most public health experts agree that unprecedented levels of overweight and obesity pose an immediate and growing threat to human health. CDC statistics show that about one in three U.S. adults are obese—they're not just fat, they're *obese*. That's 72 million people! Millions more are considered significantly overweight. In fact, less than one-third of American adults are currently at a healthy weight. That means the number of supersized people in the United

States today outnumbers (and by far outweighs) the number of normal-sized people. While obesity is difficult to define in children because they are still growing, there has been nearly a four-fold increase in childhood obesity since 1970. At least one in five children are currently overweight, and 80 percent of children who are overweight as adolescents become obese by age twenty-five. Yikes!

True *Effing Fact

The Skinny on Being Fat
Being significantly overweight or obese increases the risk of premature death, heart attack, heart disease, stroke, high blood pressure, peripheral vascular disease, diabetes, post-menopausal breast cancer, colon cancer, gallbladder cancer, uterine cancer, dementia, Alzheimer's disease, arthritis, infertility, and kidney failure.

Americans spend $47 million each year on Twinkies and $36 billion each year on pizza. That's quite a lot of dough. But can you believe Americans spend much more on diet products? In fact, we spend more money on diet products than all those pizzas and Twinkies combined. That's right—according to the most recent statistics compiled by the American Dietetic Association the United States spends more than $68 *billion* on diet programs and products from Atkins, Jenny Craig, South Beach, Slim-Fast, and Nutrisystem, and on pills like Alli, SlimQuick, and Hydroxycut. At any given time, approximately one in four American women are on a diet, and so are one in six American men. Many of them jump from diet to diet like strung-out junkies searching for their next flab fix.

But take a look around and take a good look in the mirror—diets don't work well for anybody, even if they are rich and famous celebrities. After losing 160 pounds, talk show host Oprah Winfrey appeared toned and trim on the January 2005 cover of *O* magazine. In 2009 she confessed to gaining most of the weight back. Actress Kirstie Alley lost seventy-five pounds by using the diet program Jenny Craig, but she regained all those pounds after three years. Ex-Dodger manager Tommy Lasorda famously trimmed down by using the diet shake Slim-Fast, and so did NFL Hall of Fame coach Bill Parcells. Both men gained all the weight back.

Diets simply do not work. Most people who initially lose weight on commercial diet programs regain one-third of the weight loss within one year, and most of them are back to their baseline weight in three to five years. That's exactly what happened to Oprah, Kirstie, Tommy, and Bill, and that's exactly what happens to nearly everyone on a diet. In fact, dieting is *so unsuccessful* that many experts put the diet failure rate at 95 percent. But we still keep trying, despite the fact that yo-yo dieting alters metabolism, making it easier to gain weight and more difficult to lose it. So why do people keep trying diet after diet and keep failing? The answer may surprise you—dieting is addictive.

Are *You* a Diet Addict?

1. Have you repeatedly tried and failed to control your weight with diets?
2. Has dieting interfered with your life, social activities, or employment?
3. Do you have constant thoughts about dieting?
4. Do you jump from diet to diet?
5. Have you ever dieted in a way that put your health in danger?

Diets can be psychologically and physically addictive. If you answered yes to two or more of the above questions, you could be a diet addict. Scientists have long known that behaviors among yo-yo dieters and relapsing drug addicts are quite similar. What drives people to alcohol and drugs in the first place drives many others to extreme diets, overeating, and other eating disorders; genetics, emotional strain, depression, peer pressure, and insecurity are just some of the reasons.

Dieters frequently lie about their food intake and often hide their diet effort—or lack of effort. Certainly, the foods in your diet can be addictive; high-fat, high-salt, and high-sugar diets have all been shown to be moderately addictive in scientific studies. The urge to diet can be so irresistible for some people that they will do destructive things to their bodies just to be slimmer; anorexia nervosa and bulimia are just two extreme examples of this behavior. Needless to say, many people abuse diuretic medicines (aka "water pills"), laxatives, and amphetamines to stay thin. Some people even continue smoking cigarettes for fear that quitting smoking will make them fatter.

Animal models suggest that repeated phases of dieting, followed by tasty food choices, results in excessive eating, weight gain, and an increase in anxiety behaviors. Does that sound familiar? It should, because the same mechanism is probably at work in people who repeatedly diet. Think about it. If you have been eating chocolate fudge cake every day for one month, it loses some of its day-to-day appeal after a while, doesn't it? Now imagine that you haven't eaten chocolate fudge cake for a month and someone offers you a piece. How does it taste then? It tastes downright delicious. When you deprive yourself of a desired food, your brain gets primed for the next food fix. This is probably an evolutionary survival reflex that kept our ancient ancestors searching for fatty, calorie-dense food when food was scarce.

But in modern times, in most places food is widely available. You starve yourself on a diet, your body thinks food is scarce, you binge on your favorite foods, and you get a pleasurable rush. You may not feel like an addict, because this is the normal eating pattern for so many Americans. Many drug addicts use drugs to feel "normal," not necessarily to get high. But that bad-food buzz becomes stronger and stronger with each subsequent diet-and-binge cycle, and that is what makes most people sabotage their own weight-loss efforts. Diets can work for some people, but only under very specific circumstances:

- Diets *do* work for short-term weight loss.

- Diets *do* work for some people who need to control their blood sugar for diabetes.

- Diets *do* work for some people who are trying to control their high blood pressure.

- Diets *do* work for some people who are trying to lower their cholesterol.

- Diets *do not* work for long-term weight loss in 95 percent of people.

THE *EFFING SOLUTION: DIET DETOX

How the United States became so fat so quickly is a bit of a medical mystery. Some experts suspect an "obesity virus" is playing a role, while others claim that fat-storing genes that protected us from famine and starvation thousands of years ago are now biologically backfiring because food is plentiful. Still others put the blame on foods containing high-fructose corn syrup, excessive carbohydrates, or excess fats. Any or all of these theories could be contributing to the obesity epidemic. We just

True *Effing Fact

What a Waist!
Belly fat, or so-called visceral fat, is the most dangerous kind of fat. Belly fat has been linked to high cholesterol, heart disease, diabetes, Alzheimer's disease, and premature death. Men with a 38-inch waist or larger and women with a 35-inch waist or larger are considered to be at high risk for these diseases.

don't have all the pieces to the puzzle yet. However, we do have the two largest pieces of the obesity puzzle, and the good news is you can completely control both of them.

Forget counting fat grams, carbs, or calculating the glycemic index of your foods. You don't have to go on

What *Really* Causes Obesity?
Too many calories consumed.
Too few calories burned.

a diet. The secret to losing weight and keeping it off is simple: just target the two biggest pieces in the puzzle. You *must* consume fewer calories than you are currently consuming, and you *must* get more physical activity than you are currently getting. That might sound like a diet to you, but it isn't. It's a *do*-it. It is the only solution. You must change how much food you are eating and how much you are moving your body, and you must change forever. There is no quick fix. Plan to see results over a long period of time. Cut back gradually. Replace high-calorie foods with healthier choices. Halve your portion sizes. Skip appetizers and desserts. Instead of three cookies each day, switch to two, then one, then one cookie every few days. Plan on going slowly, and plan on being frustrated. Relapsing into old yo-yo dieting habits is common. The lure is hard to resist, but stick with it. According to the National Weight Control Registry (NWCR), considered to be the largest and most authoritative study on successful long-term weight loss, people who lose weight and keep it off usually share these six features:

Six Slimming Success Secrets

- They eat breakfast every day.
- They watch very little television.
- They maintain a low-calorie, low-fat diet.
- They exercise, on average, one hour a day.
- They weigh themselves frequently.
- They maintain a high level of dietary restraint.

The NWCR research also found that guidance from a licensed clinical nutritionist can help keep those extra pounds from coming back. So if you really want to break your dieting addiction, talk to a nutritionist, start eating healthier foods, and watch your calories and portion sizes. Begin your day with a healthy breakfast, get on the scale at least once a week, turn off the television, and take a walk—or better yet, take a hike. Hiking burns 480 calories in one hour—that's enough to burn off one quarter-pound hamburger.

True *Effing Fact

Diet Don't Buy It!

There is little scientific evidence that diet foods and artificially sweetened beverages help people lose a lot of weight. They may even pack on a few pounds. Scientists at Purdue University found that when lab rats are fed artificially sweetened diet beverages they eat more food to compensate for the lost calories. And several studies have found that when food is labeled as being low-fat or reduced-calorie, people eat roughly 50 percent more calories.

THE #2 *EFFING PROBLEM: INACTIVITY

When was the last time you took the stairs for more than a few flights? Or walked to work? If you're like most Americans, you've rarely done either. But your grandparents or great-grandparents probably did just that, and many of them did it on a daily basis. One of the largest factors contributing to rising U.S. obesity levels is a decrease in general physical activity. Notice that the real *effing problem is not simply a lack of exercise, but *inactivity*.

Statistics from the Centers for Disease Control suggest that more than half of U.S. adults are not getting enough daily physical activity for good health, and one in four adults are not active at all during their leisure time. Today's children are even less active than their parents, because few of them engage in formal exercise. Physical education classes in many schools have been scaled back or abandoned, and the result is that two-thirds of U.S. students do not participate in daily PE classes. And playtime has changed dramatically. Hide-and-seek has been replaced by *Guitar Hero* and *Mortal Kombat*.

Getting daily exercise is indeed extremely important. But exercise is just one very specific form of physical activity. Other forms of physical activity seem to be equally important for optimal health. Unfortunately, all forms of physical activity, formal and informal, are on the decline. Automation in the workplace, computers, increased reliance on automobiles and mass transit, less leisure time, video games, television, and other entertainment options are all probably playing a significant role in making us fatter.

Relying exclusively on formal exercise to counteract the decrease in activity is a common health pitfall. For most people, getting one hour of daily formal exercise at the gym will not off-set seven hours of sleeping, eight hours of sitting at a work desk, two hours of sitting down at meals, one hour of sitting in the car commuting, and another three hours sitting on the couch watching television. To think that one hour at the gym will offset twenty-three hours of inactivity is absurd. Previous generations were a lot more physically active throughout the entire day, and you need to incorporate some of those Old World ways into your new way of life.

But you really can make a big difference in your health by making tiny physical efforts throughout the day. A study published in the *Journal of the American Medical Association* in 1999 found that increasing life-style activities was just as

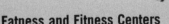

True *Effing Fact

Fatness and Fitness Centers
There are more fitness centers in the United States than ever before. The International Health Racquet and Sportsclub Association (IHRSA) claims there were more than 41.5 million U.S. gym memberships in 2008.
The IHRSA also reports a 231 percent increase in "frequent" or "core" gym users from 1987–2007. During the same time period, obesity skyrocketed to record levels.

effective as taking step aerobics. Both regimens in the study included a low-fat, low-calorie diet, but after sixteen weeks, the two groups lost the same amount of weight and had similar improvements in blood pressure and cholesterol levels.

The *Effing Solution: Become an Everyday Action Hero

So how do you incorporate more physical activity into each of your days? It's simple—and it can be a lot of fun. Of course, you should be walking as often as possible, and try taking the stairs instead of the elevator, but it is imperative to be more imaginative. Instead of buying bread, make the dough from scratch and knead it. Buy cookie batter and mix it by hand. Go dancing on a date instead of going out to the movies, or go to a cooking class instead of a restaurant. Park in spots far away from stores and walk. Take tennis lessons. Wash windows, mop, or sweep the floors. Gardening can be a physically demanding hobby, but it is rewarding. Go sailing or rowing instead of motorboating. Play outdoors with the kids or the pets. Chop firewood. Paint the rooms in your house instead of hiring a painting crew. Volunteer to clean up streets or parks in your neighborhood. Join a hiking club or a sports team. Have sex more often. There are many ways to increase the amount of action in your life. Look for ways you can creatively add some physicality to your daily routine. And remember: all these activities also keep you from snacking.

Housework Workout

The American Council for Fitness and Nutrition estimates the amount of calories spent per 30 minutes of activity:

Brisk walk = 150 calories (or one Twinkie)

Gardening = 150 calories
Raking leaves = 150 calories
Shoveling snow = 300 calories (or two Twinkies!)
Vacuuming = 100 calories
Washing windows = 100 calories
Sweeping = 100 calories

Formal exercise is important, too. Regular exercise can improve mood, help alleviate depression, lower high blood pressure, and lower high cholesterol. It also fights heart disease, diabetes, dementia, and Alzheimer's disease, and helps lower the risk of several types of cancer. Make time for exercise; it needs to be a priority. People who exercise daily are not any different from anybody else. They decided to commit to an exercise plan, and they did not give up. That is the one story all daily exercisers have in common. It could be your story too. Don't allow the internal enemy to tell you that you don't have the time to exercise. Several studies have proven that daily exercise helps people manage their time better, think better, and feel better. Exercise becomes easier each day, and it is one of the best-known ways to relieve stress.

So how much formal exercise should you be getting? The American College of Sports Medicine and the American Heart Association recommend weight training at least twice a week, along with at least thirty minutes of moderate cardiovascular exercise each day for adults. Moderate intensity is recommended over vigorous exercise, because you can exercise for a longer period of time, and some experts believe it might help you burn more fat.

The Talk Test

Don't know the difference between low-intensity, moderate, and vigorous exercise? The "talk test" is a very reliable way of measuring exercise intensity.

Low Intensity: You can easily complete sentences. Work harder!

Moderate Intensity: Slightly breathless, can speak a few words, sentences are difficult. You are close to your target heart rate and in the "fat-burning zone."

High Intensity: You cannot talk. You are exercising too hard! Slow down!

THE #3 *EFFING PROBLEM: YOU'RE STILL SMOKING

Even if you do not smoke, continue to read this section. It might help you convince someone else to stop smoking. Cigarette smoking is the single largest preventable cause of disease and premature death worldwide. Roughly 43.4 million Americans still smoke; that's about one in five people.* This year 443,000 people will die due to smoking-related illnesses, according to the CDC. That figure is about the same number of people

---

*These numbers are actually an improvement. In November of 2008 the Centers for Disease Control reported that the number of current smokers in the U.S. had dipped just below 20 percent for the first time on record.

in seven NFL football stadiums filled to capacity—with one person dying every 72 seconds throughout the year. It's like having a 9/11–style terrorist attack every three days. And for every death due to tobacco smoke, twenty more people are suffering from at least one serious illness related to smoking. There is no debate: smoking cigarettes is a disease-causing, life-shortening habit.

Cigarette smoke is toxic to almost every organ in the human body. The risk of damage, disease, and death is directly related to the number of cigarettes smoked per day and the number of years spent smoking them. And the harmful effects of smoking are not limited to the smoker. Each year exposure to secondhand smoke causes 3,400 lung cancer deaths in nonsmoking adults, as well as 22,700–69,600 deaths due to heart disease. Based on those statistics, it is probable that secondhand smoke kills more adults each year than breast cancer. But young children and infants are also vulnerable to the effects of secondhand smoke, because their lungs are still developing. The American Lung Association estimates that secondhand smoke causes between 150,000 and 300,000 lower respiratory tract infections in young children and infants each year, and 430 deaths from sudden infant death syndrome (SIDS).

True *Effing Fact

Up in Smoke

There are more than 4,000 chemicals in tobacco smoke—such as radioactive polonium-210, nickel, formaldehyde, cadmium, and benzene—and at least 60 of them are known to cause cancer. Cigarette smoke also contains the poisons arsenic, carbon monoxide, and lead.

Here's what happens when you smoke just one cigarette. From the second you light up and inhale, the tobacco smoke coats your tongue, your gums, and the mucous membranes of your mouth with poisons like formaldehyde, ammonia, and vinyl chloride. As the smoke fills the airways, it paralyzes a large portion of the lung clearance system, making you more susceptible to colds, pneumonia, and other infections. The poison carbon monoxide seeps into your bloodstream, making it more difficult for your red blood cells to carry oxygen. Your respiratory rate increases, and it becomes more difficult to take a full breath.

True *Effing Fact

Fuming Madness
The Office of the Surgeon General says there is no safe level of exposure to secondhand smoke for children, and even brief exposures at low levels can cause harm. But still, almost 60 percent of children under age eleven are exposed to secondhand smoke. That's 22 million kids!

At the same time, nicotine and other chemicals are also seeping from the lungs into your bloodstream, causing your heart rate to increase by about 30 percent and raising your blood pressure. Blood vessels throughout the body constrict, depriving your organs of vital oxygen and exposing them to toxins. In the skin, the constriction of blood vessels causes your complexion to take on a sickly gray appearance, and over time it causes wrinkles.

What's Your Smoke Age?

Habitual smoking can make a person's face look twenty years older. A 2007 study published in the *Archives of Dermatology* found smokers had significantly more fine lines and wrinkles than nonsmokers—but not just on the face. Smoking accelerated skin aging even in skin areas that were not exposed to the sun.

Lung cancer is the leading cancer killer of both men and women in the United States, and smoking cigarettes causes nearly 90 percent of all lung cancer deaths. Men who smoke are twenty-three times more likely to develop lung cancer than men who do not smoke, and women smokers are thirteen times more likely to develop the deadly disease. In 2008 the American Cancer Society (ACS) estimated that 215,020 Americans were diagnosed with lung cancer and another 161,840 were killed by it. Lung cancer kills with assembly line precision, and very few people beat it. Smoking also causes most cases of oral cancer, throat cancer, laryngeal cancer, and bladder cancer, and it is a major risk factor for kidney cancer, pancreatic cancer, cervical cancer, and a form of cancer called acute myeloid leukemia (AML).

Damage to the lungs is extensive. Smokers are more prone to bronchitis and pneumonia, and the infections tend to be more severe. In teenagers and adolescents, tobacco smoke can prevent their lungs from developing fully. Smoking cigarettes is also the single biggest risk factor for emphysema or chronic obstructive pulmonary disease (COPD), a progressive and incurable condition where the tiny air sacs in the lungs are destroyed. Many COPD sufferers become dependent on supplemental oxygen and struggle for every breath.

Smoking can lead to almost any kind of heart disease. Cigarette smoke makes the blood more prone to clotting, and it causes fatty plaques to build up in the walls of the coronary arteries. This is a condition called atherosclerosis. Due to carbon monoxide in the bloodstream and damage to the lung tissue, the heart muscle receives less oxygen so it has to work harder to supply the rest of the body. That raises blood pressure, and over time often leads to congestive heart failure. Smokers are two to four times more likely to develop heart disease than nonsmokers, and they are at twice the risk of sudden cardiac death.

Smoking causes brain damage. While many smokers say they feel more mentally alert after having a cigarette, research shows that smoking cigarettes might actually make you dumber. A study from Scottish researchers found that current smokers performed worse on five tests of mental ability compared to nonsmokers, suggesting that the habit is lowering their IQs. Smokers are more likely to experience rapid mental decline as they grow older, and one study found that the rate of mental decline was five times faster in elderly smokers compared to nonsmokers.

Smokers are more likely to develop Alzheimer's disease and other forms of dementia. Other studies have shown that smoking cigarettes can permanently alter the balance of feel-good chemicals in the brain, and female smokers have been shown to be at increased risk of depression. Smoking increases the brain damage seen in alcoholics and more than doubles the risk of having a stroke.

Smoking speeds up the aging process throughout the entire body, but nowhere is it more apparent than on the skin. In fact, the only thing that ages the skin more quickly than cigarettes is the sun. Cigarette smoke decreases the blood flow to the outermost layers of the skin, giving it a gray, pale, and thin appearance. Collagen production is also decreased. Over time both processes lead to accelerated skin aging. Plus, smokers often purse their lips to smoke or squint, and this is believed to worsen the wrinkles. These skin changes associated with cigarettes are most noticeable in people who have smoked for longer than ten years, and while they are not deadly, the changes may be irreversible, even if you stop smoking.

True *Effing Fact

Deadly Spread

Roughly 25 percent of all lung cancer tumors will spread to the brain, and at that point, the median survival is just three to six months.

Smoking just a few cigarettes reduces blood flow to the penis and prevents men from achieving a full erection. The nicotine in the cigarette smoke causes the arteries to constrict. Over time smoking permanently damages these arteries, and it leads to erectile dysfunction. Through other mechanisms nicotine and the carbon monoxide in cigarette smoke also lower the male sex hormone testosterone. In fact, studies have shown that men who smoke are about 40 percent more likely to suffer from impotence, have poorer semen quality, and a decreased sperm count.

Cigarette Shrinkage

A 1998 study conducted by a researcher at Boston University suggested long-term smoking decreases the size of a man's penis.

Cigarettes can have a huge impact on a woman's sex life, too.
During sexual arousal the clitoris and vagina normally swell. In
women who smoke, this response is diminished and they have a
more difficult time achieving orgasm. Cigarette smoke also
interferes with production of ovarian hormones, which can lead
to menstrual abnormalities. Female smokers have a harder time
conceiving children, about a 40 percent lower chance of concep-
tion with each cycle compared to nonsmoking women. Women
who smoke while taking oral contraceptives are also twenty
times more likely to develop serious blood clots. Smoking
increases the risk of premature birth, low birth weight, birth
defects, and sudden infant death syndrome.

It's important to mention the dangers of secondhand smoke.
Though some experts believe the risks are overblown, studies
have shown that nonsmokers who live with a smoker are 25–30
percent more likely to develop heart disease and 20–30 percent
more likely to develop lung cancer. Each year in the U.S. secondhand smoke causes 3,500 deaths due to lung cancer and more
than 22,000 deaths due to heart disease.

The Hook

A study published in the *Archives of Pediatric and Adolescent Medicine* found that one in ten youths who smoke cigarettes are "hooked" on nicotine within two days of trying their very first cigarette. One in four is addicted within one month. Canadian researchers say some people can be hooked after their very first smoke. They suspect there may be different susceptibilities in the brain's reward center.

THE *EFFING SOLUTION: HOW TO BUTT OUT

Quitting smoking can be very difficult, and very few people are successful on their first try. So if you tried to quit before and you failed, don't be discouraged—keep trying, because quitting smoking will help your health immediately. Just twenty minutes after your last cigarette, your blood vessels relax and your blood pressure returns to its normal level. Within eight hours the oxygen level in your bloodstream also normalizes. Twenty-four hours later the carbon monoxide levels in the lungs plummet, and over the next few days the mucous will loosen in the airways, making breathing easier. In a few weeks your circulation will improve; so will your sense of smell and taste.

In one year the risk of heart attack is cut in half compared to people who are still smoking. Each year you remain smoke free, your risk of developing cancer or heart disease from smoking decreases even further. The Harvard School of Public Health found that within five years of quitting smoking, the overall risk of death is reduced by 13 percent. The risk of dying from stroke drops by more than 27 percent, and the risk of dying from heart disease is reduced by 47 percent.

Quitting cigarettes is going to be difficult, and failing several times is the norm. Nicotine is highly addictive, and it's important to keep your expectations in check. About 5 percent of people are successful on any given attempt, according to the American Cancer Society. The more you try, the more likely you are to succeed. Sometimes smokers need to try eight to ten times before they have success. Accept the possibility of failure and resign yourself to trying several times until you break the habit for good. This will keep you from getting discouraged. Involve your healthcare provider. There are many ways to quit smoking, and there is really no way to tell which method will work best for you. You might have to try several methods before finding one that works, and your healthcare provider can help individualize your treatment.

Prepare yourself for the withdrawal. While some smokers have very mild withdrawal, other smokers have more significant

True *Effing Fact

Never Too Late
It's never too late to quit smoking. Studies have shown that people over age sixty-five who have been smoking for decades can still add years to their lives by quitting. Even older smokers with heart disease can benefit.

symptoms. Most longtime smokers will experience some kind of withdrawal within a few hours of their last cigarette, and typically the peak intensity of their withdrawal will come two to three days after quitting.

Possible Symptoms of Nicotine Withdrawal:
Cravings for cigarettes
Irritability, anger, and anxiety
Dizziness
Headaches
Difficulty concentrating
Increased appetite
Difficulty sleeping

Step 1: Support

It's important to have your friends and family support your decision to quit. The American Cancer Society has also established a Quitline in many U.S. states. Specialized counselors can answer most questions about quitting cigarettes and help you choose the best smoking cessation method. Studies have shown that smokers who use telephone counseling are twice as likely to quit compared to those who do not receive counseling. Some studies have also shown that joining a support group might increase your chances of quitting for good.

Commit yourself to quitting. Pick a quit date. Pick a method of smoking cessation and stick to it. If you fail, don't get discouraged; that's normal. Just try it again or switch to another method. The ACS has some very valuable tips on how to do this successfully.

Step 2: The Methods

Cold turkey. Quitting cold turkey is probably the most popular method of smoking cessation, but it is also probably the least effective. A recent analysis of sixty-nine studies on smoking cessation found that nicotine replacement therapy (NRT) and smoking cessation medications are about twice as effective as going cold turkey. But no doubt the cold turkey approach will work for some people. Research has shown that younger smokers tend to be more successful at quitting cold turkey than older smokers, and men are more successful at this method of quitting than women.

True *Effing* Fact

Younger smokers and men seem to have the most success with the cold turkey method.

Cold Turkey

Some experts say the origin of the phrase "cold turkey" dates back to the 1920s and refers to heroin withdrawal. When an addict is withdrawing from heroin, the blood flow is directed to the internal organs, leaving the skin white and goose bumped, like the skin of a cold turkey.

Nicotine replacement therapy (NRT). There are various methods of nicotine replacement therapy. NRT delivers nicotine in the form of gum, sprays, lozenges, patches, inhalers, wafers, lollipops, and even lip balm, and it helps reduce cravings and physical withdrawal symptoms. When NRT is combined with some kind of psychological support, it doubles the chances of kicking the habit.

But this therapy is not for everyone. People with heart disease should not try NRT without talking to their doctor and neither should pregnant women or women who are trying to become pregnant. The nicotine in NRT may complicate pregnancy, and it may pose a risk to the unborn baby. People who smoke less than half a pack a day may also not benefit, and they might want to speak to their doctor about a lower-dose NRT. But for many smoking adults, choosing a method of NRT is a really good starting point. NRT is most effective when started in the first few days of quitting, and many times it is combined with other methods.

Chew on This

Nicotine replacement therapy is only intended for short-term use. Nicotine raises blood pressure and raises cancer risk. A 2008 study led by London researchers found that prolonged use of nicotine lozenges, gum, or inhalers can lead to mutations in DNA and potentially raise the risk of oral cancers.

Prescription medications. Bupropion, marketed as Zyban for smoking cessation, is the same prescription medication found in the antidepressant Wellbutrin. It comes in pill form and is taken once or twice a day. Bupropion does not contain any nicotine, and it reduces cravings for cigarettes by altering chemicals inside the brain. It may also block the effects of nicotine in the brain. It has been shown to lessen some of the nicotine withdrawal symptoms, such as irritability, anxiety, and restlessness. Bupropion works best if started within two weeks of quitting cigarettes. Many start taking bupropion while they are still smoking so that the medication can reach a therapeutic level before their quit date. Some studies have shown that the drug roughly doubles the quit rate at three months. That's fairly effective. Bupropion is often combined with NRT methods. The drug can lower the seizure threshold, and it is not recommended for people who have had a history of seizures, heavy alcohol consumption, serious head injury, bipolar disorder, anorexia nervosa, or bulimia.

True *Effing Fact

Unlike many other psychiatric drugs, and nearly all antidepressant medications, bupropion does not cause weight gain or sexual dysfunction.

Varenicline, sold as Chantix, is a newer prescription medication that works inside the brain by binding to the nicotine receptors. By blocking the effects of nicotine, the drug helps reduce cravings and negates some of the pleasurable effects of smoking cigarettes. Like bupropion, evidence suggests that varenicline doubles the chances of quitting successfully. Some studies have shown that it may be superior to bupropion in short-term quitting success. It comes in pill form, and the dose is gradually increased until one pill is taken twice a day. Treatment lasts twelve weeks. But if the smoker is successful at twelve weeks of varenicline therapy, another twelve weeks of treatment might increase the chances of quitting for good. People who use this drug in conjunction with NRT may experience an increase in side effects, such as nausea and headaches, and it is generally not recommended.

A word of caution: There have recently been a lot of reports about depression and suicidal thoughts occurring while people are taking varenicline or bupropion. If you are taking either of these prescription medications and start experiencing abnormal thoughts, consult your doctor immediately.

Troubling Side Effects

Like all medications, bupropion and varenicline can have serious side effects in some users. The reported psychiatric side effects of these medicines are particularly troubling and may include:

Suicidal thoughts
Suicidal actions
Mood swings
Aggression or hostility
Depression
Agitation

Getting to the point. Acupuncture is a form of ancient Chinese medicine where long, thin needles are inserted at specific points of the skin to treat a variety of medical conditions. While some studies have shown it can help minimize the withdrawal symptoms associated with smoking cessation, others have not. And when a large analysis of all the studies was performed, there was no evidence that acupuncture was more effective at reducing withdrawal symptoms than a placebo. There is even less evidence to support the use of laser acupuncture for smoking cessation. However, many smokers have had success with acupuncture and laser acupuncture, and it might be worth exploring for some people.

Hypnosis. Some people find hypnosis useful, and some studies have suggested it might help people who are trying to quit smoking. But there is a lot of variability in hypnosis techniques, and there is currently not enough evidence to support its widespread use as a smoking cessation treatment. However, like acupuncture, some smokers will have success with hypnosis; it is harmless, and they should not be discouraged from giving it a try.

THE #4 *EFFING PROBLEM: YOU'RE DRINKING EXCESS ALCOHOL

Drinking moderate amounts of alcohol is often touted as a healthy habit, but alcohol is a potent drug. In fact, alcohol is the most commonly abused drug in the world, and it is clearly the drug of choice in the United States. Roughly 61 percent of American adults drink alcohol at least on occasion according to the CDC, and many of them drink alcohol in excess. Nearly 18 million Americans meet the diagnostic criteria for having alcoholism or another alcohol abuse disorder.

True *Effing Fact

Celebrity Rehab

What do Joseph Stalin, Ulysses S. Grant, Edgar Allan Poe, Wonder Woman star Lynda Carter, astronaut Buzz Aldrin, golfer John Daly, Ernest Hemingway, Lindsay Lohan, Mel Gibson, Jack Kerouac, Robin Williams, Jimi Hendrix, and writer Stephen King all have in common? They all struggled with alcoholism.

Over time alcohol abuse can permanently damage the heart, shrink the brain, scar the liver, inflame the pancreas, and injure other internal organs. Alcohol is also listed as a "known carcinogen" by the U.S. Department of Health and Human Services. Excess alcohol consumption raises the risk of several types of cancer, including breast cancer, colon cancer, throat cancer, and oral cancer. Alcohol is known to worsen diabetes, high blood pressure, and gastritis. It also causes erectile dysfunction in men, menstrual abnormalities in women, and birth defects in unborn babies. Plus, it makes people fat. As a result of all this drinking, there are more than 120,000 alcohol-related deaths each year in the United States, and every thirty minutes a driver impaired by alcohol kills someone on our streets.

Alcohol can also have an effect on health through its interactions with medications. Many medications interact with alcohol even at low to moderate levels of drinking. Sometimes these interactions render the medication ineffective, while at other times alcohol can enhance the effect of the drug with possible deadly consequences. Some medications, like cough syrups and laxatives, can contain as much as 10 percent alcohol themselves.

If you are taking any medication for any reason, it is probably best to refrain from alcohol entirely.

Higher Intelligence?

Highly intelligent children may be more at risk for alcohol abuse disorders later on in life. A British study found children who had a high IQ at age ten drank more alcohol at age thirty when compared to children who were less intellectually gifted. Highly intelligent kids were also more likely to develop problems with alcohol as adults.

Alcoholism is a treatable chronic disease marked by a strong physical and psychological need for alcohol. Both genetic and environmental influences are thought to play important roles in causing the condition, and alcoholics are powerless over their addiction. However, drinkers who meet the criteria for "alcohol abuse" disorders have not lost complete control of their drinking—they are not yet addicted, but they drink to such an extent that it has a significant negative impact on other aspects of their lives. Alcohol abuse disorders often lead to alcoholism, and all people with alcoholism abuse alcohol. So how do you know if you have a problem with alcohol? If you answer yes to any of the following questions, you might have a problem, and it is time to talk to your doctor about your drinking.

Do You Have a Problem with Alcohol?

1. Do you ever drink alone or in secret?
2. Have you ever blacked out or not recalled events while drinking?
3. Do you have trouble limiting the amount of alcohol you drink?
4. Have you tried to quit drinking?
5. Do you get annoyed when people criticize your drinking?
6. Do you feel irritable if you have no alcohol?
7. Have you had legal, relationship, or employment problems because of your drinking?
8. Do you experience physical withdrawal when you don't have any alcohol?

But isn't alcohol good for you? Several studies have shown that moderate alcohol consumption is associated with a lower risk of heart disease, stroke, and possibly dementia. This is because many alcoholic beverages contain plant compounds called flavonoids, which help maintain the elasticity of blood vessels and prevent the arteries from stiffening with age. Red wine, in particular, is also high in a compound called resveratrol, which is currently being studied for possible antiaging and medicinal properties. Most people who drink do not drink moderately. Moderation means one serving of alcohol per day for women, regardless if it comes from wine, beer, or spirits, and two to three servings a day for men. The research is clear: if you are drinking more than moderately, or if you are binge drinking on the weekends, you are doing more harm than good.

THE *EFFING SOLUTION: HOW TO CUT BACK OR QUIT

Denial is very common among people with alcoholism and other alcohol abuse disorders. Many alcohol abusers and alcoholics won't seek help until they run into legal problems or develop a pressing health issue. Accepting that you have a problem with alcohol is a critical first step to breaking the addiction. But first a word of caution about quitting alcohol cold turkey: Some heavy drinkers who suddenly stop drinking alcohol will suffer an acute, potentially life-threatening withdrawal syndrome known as delirium tremens (DTs). This condition is marked by an internal tremulousness, irritation, confusion, and in many cases, seizures. So if you have been a heavy drinker for a long time, it is imperative that you seek professional medical help.

Step 1: Admit, Get Support, Get Help

There are four main elements to effective treatment of alcoholism. The first element is being a willing participant. If the alcoholic or alcohol abuser does not want to be helped, there is little chance any method will be successful. The second element is assembling a social support system. This could be family, a group of friends, a 12-step program, or a support group. You must be able to discuss your alcohol problem openly

True *Effing Fact

Habitual heavy drinkers should not quit alcohol abruptly. A serious and potentially fatal withdrawal syndrome called delirium tremens (DTs) may result. Medical assistance is required.

and without judgment. It is essential to build a social safety net to prevent relapse. The third element is psychological counseling. Most alcoholics and alcohol abusers have unresolved psychological issues that play a role in their drinking. Plus, studies have shown that family counseling and individual counseling can help increase long-term alcohol quit rates. And the fourth element is medical therapy. Not everyone with an alcohol problem will need to be treated with prescription medications, but many alcoholics will benefit from having medical therapy. Since alcohol is toxic to the body, it is recommended that all problem drinkers receive a thorough physical examination and some blood work.

Step 2: The Methods

Twelve steps. Alcoholics Anonymous (AA) is the original 12-step facilitation program. It is described as a worldwide fellowship of men and women who share the desire to stop drinking alcohol. It was cofounded in 1934 by Bill Wilson (aka Bill W.) after he had ruined a promising Wall Street career due to his alcohol addiction. AA is a spiritually based 12-step program that involves attending meetings, admitting powerlessness over alcohol, taking a moral inventory, making amends, and asking for assistance from God. It advocates complete abstinence from alcohol. There is a fairly high dropout rate with AA, but those who stay with the program longer are more likely to break the addiction. Many studies have shown that attending AA meetings can increase abstinence levels, but other studies have not. Some have even shown poorer outcomes among AA attendees. But for some alcoholics, joining AA will no

> **To find an Alcoholics Anonymous meeting near you, visit www.aa.org.**

> **To find a Secular Organization for Sobriety, visit www.secularsobriety.org.**

doubt save their lives—and you might be one of them. There are also 12-step facilitation programs of a more secular nature, specifically, Secular Organizations for Sobriety (SOS).

Moderation Management. The Moderation Management (MM) movement grew out of a need to treat problem drinkers who have not yet progressed to alcoholism. It does not require abstinence from alcohol. MM programs aim to change behaviors and the drinker's relationship with alcohol. It has a nine-step program that includes setting limits on moderate drinking, drink-monitoring exercises, self-management, and goal setting. Unlike AA, it is not a spiritually based program.

> **To find a Moderation Management organization, visit www.moderation.org.**

Medications. There are several medications that have been shown to help people quit drinking alcohol. Disulfiram (Antabuse) is a pill that reacts with alcohol and causes headache, flushing, nausea, and vomiting. It won't stop the cravings for alcohol, but it certainly makes drinking alcohol unpleasant. Naltrexone (ReVia or Vivitrol) has been used in the treatment of drug addiction. It appears to block neurotransmitters in the brain and prevents the "high" associated with getting drunk. Acamprosate (Campral) helps decrease the cravings for alcohol. Many times doctors will also prescribe antianxiety drugs called benzodiazepines to help minimize symptoms of alcohol withdrawal. Drugs in the benzodiazepine family include diazepam (Valium), lorazepam (Ativan), and clonazepam (Klonopin). Chlordiazepoxide (Librium) is a derivative of the benzodiazepine drugs and is also frequently used in the treatment of alcohol withdrawal. Multivitamins are often used to treat alcohol-related vitamin deficiencies.

Talk therapy. Cognitive behavioral therapy (CBT) is a form of psychotherapy that is based on the assumption that a person's own thoughts lie at the core of the psychological dysfunction, not external influences or circumstances. People often cannot change their circumstances, but they usually can change their reactions to their circumstances, and that is the basis for CBT. In treating alcoholism, the dysfunctional thoughts that led to alcoholism or alcohol abuse are examined and then replaced with more effective coping skills and functional thoughts. The treatment is usually short-term, about twenty sessions with a therapist. Some studies have suggested that CBT works as well as other forms of psychotherapy and 12-step facilitation programs for recovery from alcoholism.

Motivational enhancement therapy (MET) is another form of psychotherapy that tries to elicit and then recruit an alcoholic's personal desire to quit drinking. The treatment does not try to guide the patient or use directives but rather attempts to harness a drinker's motivations and desire for change. MET appears to be as effective as CBT or 12-step facilitation.

Although relapses are common, quitting alcohol appears to be significantly less difficult than quitting cigarettes. One-year abstinence rates of 30–60 percent have been reported through psychosocial interventions alone. Combinations of a psychotherapeutic approach, a 12-step facilitation program, and medical treatment result in the highest abstinence rates at one year and the highest likelihood of long-term abstinence.

THE #5 *EFFING PROBLEM: YOU'RE HAVING RISKY SEX

Sexually transmitted diseases (STDs) are a pressing global public health threat. There are approximately 19 million new cases of STDs diagnosed each year in the United States, and millions more go undiagnosed. In 2008 there were more than 1 million cases of chlamydia diagnosed in the United States, the largest number ever reported, and yet the CDC estimates an additional 1.7 million were infected and unaware. There were also 336,742 new cases of gonorrhea, about 40,000 new cases of HIV, and more than 1.1 million Americans were thought to be living with HIV/AIDS. Syphilis is on the rise, particularly among men who have sex with men (MSM); more than 13,500 new cases were reported in 2008. At any given time, roughly 650,000 women have bacterial vaginosis, and more than 45 million people over age twelve have a case of genital herpes. That is one in every five adolescents or adults.

Risky sex is underlying the continued spread of these dangerous and sometimes deadly diseases. Roughly half of the 19 million new STD infections each year occur in young adults aged 15–24, according to CDC statistics, and one in four sexually active teenagers contract an STD each year. Why is the rate so high? The CDC found that about half of all high school students admitted having sexual intercourse with a member of the opposite sex, and 15 percent of students admitted having sex with more than four partners. More than half of high school girls and boys have had oral sex, and slightly more than one in ten have had anal sex with a member of the opposite sex. Three percent of male high school students have had anal sex with another male. Adolescents and teens are also more likely to engage in other kinds of high-risk activities, like having

True *Effing Fact

It Can Happen to You

Adolf Hitler, Napoléon Bonaparte, Ivan the Terrible, King Henry VIII, Friedrich Nietzsche, John Keats, Leo Tolstoy, Vincent van Gogh, and Oscar Wilde all suffered from syphilis. Notorious gangster Al Capone, actor Maurice Barrymore, writer Guy de Maupassant, composer Franz Schubert, and painters Paul Gauguin, Henri de Toulouse-Lautrec, and Édouard Manet all died from syphilis.

unprotected sex while being under the influence of drugs or alcohol. More than half (53 percent) of boys say they do not use condoms every time they have sexual intercourse, and two-thirds of girls say a condom is not used every time.

But teens and adolescents are not the only ones engaging in risky sex practices. Young adults actually use condoms more consistently than older adults. More than 60 percent of people over the age of sixty are having sex at least once a month.

True*Effing Fact

One in four sexually active teens is infected with an STD each year.

Barrier methods of protection are rarely used in this older age group because the women are no longer fertile and they feel immune to the risk. But being older may make your body more susceptible to contracting a sexually transmitted disease. Seniors are not routinely screened for STDs, and many do not know they are infected. They also have less effective immune systems, and the thinner vaginal wall in older women is more likely to tear during intercourse, making transmission of HIV easier. As a result, STD rates in people over the age of forty-five have doubled over the last two decades, and people over age fifty are one of the fastest growing subgroups of new HIV infections.

Risky Sex Not Worth the Risk

Chlamydia: Like gonorrhea, chlamydia can cause pelvic inflammatory disease (PID) and raise the risk of potentially fatal ectopic pregnancies by spreading throughout a woman's uterus and fallopian tubes. PID is one of the most common causes of infertility. Women with chlamydia are five times more likely to be infected with HIV. In men, chlamydia causes few symptoms, and most men never know they are infected.

Gonorrhea: In women, gonorrhea is a common cause of PID. PID frequently leads to infertility and raises the risk of ectopic pregnancy. In men gonorrhea can result in sterility by infecting the sperm-producing tissues of the testicles. In both sexes gonorrhea increases the risk of contracting HIV, and it can spread to the joints or blood and cause a fatal infection.

Hepatitis A, B, C: Three strains of the hepatitis virus can be transmitted during sexual activity. Hepatitis B is the most common and usually the most serious. It can result in liver scarring, liver failure, and death.

Herpes: Herpes is incurable, and it can cause recurrent painful genital sores. For pregnant women, herpes can lead to serious and potentially fatal infections in their babies. Herpes makes both men and women more susceptible to HIV infection.

Human Papillomavirus (HPV): HPV commonly causes genital warts. But in women the virus causes at least 90 percent of the cases of cervical cancer. HPV also causes penile cancer in men. HPV infections are causing more rectal cancers and throat cancers due to increases in risky sex practices like anal sex and oral sex. In fact, having more than six oral sex partners in a lifetime raises the risk of oral cancer by 250 percent.

Syphilis: If left untreated, syphilis can damage the liver, joints, brain, heart, nerves, eyes, blood vessels, and bones. Pregnant women can also pass syphilis to their babies.

Sexually transmitted infections are not the only consequence of risky sex practices. Unprotected sex often leads to unintended pregnancy. According to the Guttmacher Institute, roughly half of all pregnancies in the United States are unintended. Unintentional pregnancy can take a toll on the health of both mother and baby. Women carrying unintended pregnancies are less likely to seek prenatal care, more likely to suffer from depression, and more likely to abuse drugs or alcohol while pregnant. As a result, babies born through an unintended pregnancy have a greater risk of being born at a low birth weight and have a higher risk of postnatal complications, a greater risk of being abused, and a higher risk of dying in the first year of life. Unintended pregnancy is also the main reason why more than one million abortions are performed in the United States each year.

THE *EFFING SOLUTION: GET PICKY, GET SCREENED, USE CONDOMS

The only sure way to avoid STDs is to not have sex. Abstaining from oral sex, anal sex, and vaginal sex is the only strategy proven to offer 100 percent protection from these traumatizing and terrible diseases. You cannot get STDs, HIV, or get pregnant from a toilet seat. Being in a long-term, monogamous relationship with an uninfected partner, using safer-sex practices, and limiting your number of sex partners are the next most effective methods of protection.

What Is Risky Sex?

1. Oral or vaginal sex without a condom.
2. Anal sex of any kind: the rectum tears easily, which makes the transmission of HIV more effective.
3. Sex with strangers.
4. Sex under the influence of drugs or alcohol.
5. Sex with a partner who is under the influence of drugs or alcohol.
6. Having sex for money.
7. Having sex with multiple partners.

Get picky. It is important to limit your total number of sex partners. In anonymous sex surveys, men report having two to four times more lifetime sexual partners than women. Some psychologists suggest this is the "Macho Man and Maiden" phenomenon, where men tend to exaggerate their sexual exploits and women tend to underreport them. Others argue that women try to count the number of sexual partners they have had, which often leads to underreporting, while men just estimate, which often leads to overreporting.

How Many Is Too Many?

True *Effing Blog Posts (from Answerbag.com). The question posted was "What is the average number of sexual partners for 26-year-old college-educated men and women in America?" These are some of the answers they received:

> "I am a 19-year-old college student who has had
> 15 partners in 3 years . . . normal?"
>
> —*Anonymous*

> "I am 25 and college-educated, and I'd say I've had between
> 30–35 [partners]. I don't know exactly. . . ."
>
> —*doubtful007*

> "I'm a university-educated 23-year-old female and have
> had 48 sexual partners."
>
> —*TaLooLaah*

> "I am a 19-year-old female in college and
> have been with 22 people . . ."
>
> —*Anonymous*

> "[I am a] 27-year-old female doctor with 0 partners.
> I'm the one that screws up the average."
>
> —*Anonymous*

A nationwide government survey by the CDC conducted in 2007 found that 29 percent of men and only 9 percent of women have had sex with more than fifteen people of the opposite sex. The median number of lifetime sex partners for heterosexual men was seven. The median number of sex partners for heterosexual women was four. For this study, the CDC surveyed more than six thousand adults of all races, ages 20–59, but many experts feel the numbers are conservative. Women with more than five sex partners are much more likely to become infected with HPV and are more likely to develop cervical cancer due to the virus. Having more than six oral sex partners triples the risk of head and neck cancer for both men and women. Alcohol dependence and alcohol abuse have been linked to higher numbers of sex partners, so cutting back on alcohol will help you from making some critical sex mistakes (see "The #4 *Effing Problem: You're Drinking Excess Alcohol" on p. 27).

Sex and the City

People living in New York City have twice the number of sex partners as the average American. The *New York Daily News* took a look at the sex lives of the *Sex and the City* characters to see how they compared to the real thing:

- In the six seasons of *Sex and the City*, the four main characters managed to bed 94 men and one woman.
- Samantha was the most prolific lover, with 41 men and 1 woman.
- Carrie hooked up with 18 men; so did Charlotte. Miranda bedded 17 men.
- Compared to the sexual patterns of a similar group of average New York women, those numbers were right on target.

Get screened. Having a frank conversation about your sexual practices with your healthcare provider is a valuable weapon against STDs. After assessing your risk, your provider can arrange testing for any of these diseases. But it is important to start a dialogue with your doctor, because few of these tests are performed on a routine basis. Anybody with a new sex partner or multiple sex partners should be screened for gonorrhea and chlamydia. Syphilis, HIV, and herpes screening are currently recommended only for those who are symptomatic or fall into specific risk categories.

Use condoms. If you are not abstaining from sexual activity, your best protection from HIV and other STDs is a male latex condom. A latex condom should be worn properly every time you have sex with a man, whether it is oral sex, vaginal sex, or anal sex.

About four in one thousand condoms fail, and usually the cause of condom failure is improper use. The most frequent errors include not leaving enough space at the tip of the condom for semen or using condoms that are ineffective because they have expired (yes, condoms have expiration dates), have been exposed to heat or sunlight, or have been torn by teeth or fingernails.

But even if condoms are used correctly 100 percent of the time, they will *not* offer complete protection. It is still possible to contract chlamydia, gonorrhea, hepatitis, herpes, HIV, HPV, syphilis, and all the other STDs while using condoms correctly and consistently. When used correctly and consistently, condoms can reduce the risk of HIV transmission from one partner to the next by approximately 80 percent. Studies have shown that condoms can similarly reduce the risk of chlamydia, gonorrhea, and trichomoniasis. Male latex condoms appear to be slightly less effective at preventing herpes infections.

Latex condoms do block the herpes virus, but lesions frequently occur in areas that are not protected by condoms. For the same reason, condoms are slightly less effective at preventing the spread of HPV between sex partners. Recently a study found that consistent and proper use of male latex condoms can reduce a woman's chances of HPV infection by 70 percent. The female condom appears to be an effective barrier against these diseases, but fewer definitive clinical trials have been performed. Remember: condoms are not perfect protection, but they are still the best protection.

Proper Condom Use

1. Check the expiration date.
2. Be careful not to tear the condom while opening the package.
3. Do not unroll the condom before putting it on the penis.
4. Press air out of the tip, leaving about one-half inch of space for the semen.
5. Hold the tip between thumb and forefinger.
6. If not circumcised, pull back the foreskin.
7. Place the condom over the head of the penis.
8. Roll the condom down completely.

ALWAYS put a condom on an erect penis.
ALWAYS use a water-based lubricant if you need extra lubrication.
NEVER use an oil-based lubricant, because they break down the latex.

THE #6 *EFFING PROBLEM: YOU'RE NOT GETTING ENOUGH SLEEP

Studies have shown that people will naturally sleep some-where between 8–9 hours each night when left uninterrupted. But the average American sleeps only 6.7 hours each night, according to a recent poll conducted by the National Sleep Foundation (NSF). Even on weekends, the average American sleeps just 7.4 hours. Our national sleep disorder is getting worse. Over the last several decades, the percentage of Americans who sleep less than 6 hours each night has steadily grown, while the per-centage of people who get more than 8 hours of sleep has steadily declined. In fact, the latest NSF poll shows that only one in four people today sleep more than 8 hours each night.

True *Effing Fact

The body has a natural tendency to fall asleep two times during the day. The first is the familiar noctur-nal period from 7:00 PM through midnight. The other occurs in the midafternoon, from 1:00–4:00 PM. Siesta anyone?

Believe it or not, nobody really knows why we sleep—even renowned sleep scientists are in the dark about this critical biological function. We do know that all animals with complex nervous systems sleep to some degree. The simple but industrious ant is known to take breaks that look a lot like sleep, and even some algae are known to have strong circadian rhythms. Yet despite the ubiquity of sleep in nature and its extensive scientific study, the reason for sleep is still shrouded in mystery. Of course, the simplest explanation would be that sleep allows the body to rest and restore itself. But the lack of sleep has surprisingly few immediate negative effects on the body. Muscles, for instance, do not need sleep; they need rest. And internal organs, such as the liver, kidneys, intestines, stomach, lungs, and pancreas, do not really seem to care if you are sleeping or not—they do their job anyway.

Some experts claim that sleep helps consolidate and organize procedural memory, which is the kind of memory needed to learn new tasks. There is some compelling evidence to support this theory. Numerous studies have shown that procedural memory is impaired early in people who are sleep-deprived, and other studies have shown that sleeping animals will mentally rehearse a newly acquired task during the dreaming phase of sleep known as rapid eye movement (REM) sleep.

Recently it was reported that sleep may act like a reset button for brain neurotransmitters and their receptors. After a good night's sleep, the brain's neurotransmitters are replenished, and their receptors are vacant and ready to be stimulated. Other experts think that sleep is just a form of brain housekeeping. The brain uses about one-fifth of the body's total energy, and as a result it generates a lot of damaging free radicals. The decreased brain activity seen during sleep may allow the brain's free radical scavengers enough time to mop up the mess made during the day.

Finally, some scientists have reported that REM sleep helps neurons make new connections while nondream sleep, called non-REM sleep, loosens older and more trivial connections. By discarding loose and fading memories, the brain makes room for new memories. All these theories are scientifically plausible, and it is unlikely that any one theory fully explains the reason for sleep. It is more likely that sleep serves several biological purposes. So while we don't know precisely why we sleep, we do know that sleep is extremely important. The lack of sleep can exact a devastating toll on the body and mind—in some cases it can even be fatal.

Inadequate sleep can have both acute and chronic effects on your health. After eighteen hours without sleep, your eyes start drooping and you begin to have difficulties with attention, concentration, and memory. Your brain tries to

True *Effing Fact

Eye-opening Sleep Statistics

Over one lifetime, the average American will sleep more than 221,920 hours. That is 9,246 days or 25.3 years spent in bed—and scientists don't know why.

jump-start itself with frequent yawning. After twenty-four hours without sleep, these problems become more pronounced. Your mind wanders, you have periods where you almost nod off completely, and your hands may shake with a fine tremor.

At the same time, the stress hormone cortisol rises in your bloodstream, and so does your blood pressure. If you were to drive a motor vehicle, your psychomotor impairment would be equal to that of someone with a blood alcohol content of .08 percent—the legal limit for a drunk driver. Like alcohol intoxication, drowsy driving slows reaction time, impairs judgment and concentration, and increases the risk of crashing. The National Highway Traffic Safety Administration estimates that this kind of drowsy driving causes more than 100,000 traffic accidents each year with 1,550 fatalities. After thirty-six hours of sleep deprivation, the psychiatric manifestations become debilitating for most people, and severe memory loss, hallucinations, paranoia, and delusions become increasingly likely.

Sleepless in San Diego

Randy Gardner holds the longest scientifically documented period of sleep deprivation. In 1964 the seventeen-year-old high school student from San Diego stayed awake for eleven days without using stimulants of any kind. Reportedly, by day three he was hallucinating and having occasional delusions.

When the loss of sleep is acute, like being out all night at a party, our bodies naturally compensate the following day by increasing the amount of time spent in sleep. But when sleep loss is chronic, the body's ability to compensate is compromised. The sleep debt persists and grows. This chronic sleep loss raises the risk of several dangerous diseases. The loss of sleep impairs glucose (sugar) metabolism, increases insulin resistance, and raises the risk of type 2 diabetes. One study conducted by the University of Chicago found that increased insulin resistance developed after just three nights of sleep deprivation was equivalent to gaining twenty to thirty pounds!

Getting less than six and a half hours of sleep each night doubles the risk of high blood pressure, which may be one of the reasons why chronic sleep loss increases the risk of heart disease. Sleep loss also raises the risk of having a heart attack. In fact, heart attacks increase by 5 percent when we "spring forward" and lose an hour of sleep for daylight savings time.

Chronic sleep loss decreases the immune system's ability to fight infections, and it raises the risk of depression and some cancers. One study found that women who slept less than seven hours each night had a 47 percent increased risk of developing cancer. In terms of cancer prevention, getting adequate sleep may be even more important than getting exercise.

Dying to Sleep

People with a rare genetic brain disorder called fatal familial insomnia lose their ability to fall asleep. Once symptoms start, survival is usually 7–18 months.

The *Effing Solution: Bedtime Basic Training

If you have chronic insomnia, it is important to find out why you are having difficulty falling asleep and to seek the appropriate help. Emotional problems like stress, anxiety, and depression account for roughly one-half of all cases of chronic insomnia. Prescription medications are a frequent but often overlooked source of sleeplessness. Sleep also changes with age. As you get older you tend to need less sleep, and your sleep is often interrupted. And, of course, an underlying sleep disorder like sleep apnea may lie at the root of your problem. It cannot be stressed enough: having persistent sleep difficulties is not normal, and if you are having trouble falling asleep or staying asleep, it is vitally important to speak with a licensed professional.

Bedtime Basic Training

1. **Establish and maintain a regular bedtime and wake time.**
   Have you ever awakened a few minutes before your alarm clock was set to go off? This happens frequently because like your alarm clock, your circadian rhythm has been programmed to that specific wake time. In a similar fashion, your body can be set to a specific bedtime. The more consistent the bedtime and wake time, the stronger the circadian rhythm is reinforced.

2. **Establish a bedtime routine.** Some people take warm baths or climb under the covers with a good book, while others

meditate or pray. Establishing these habitual bedtime routines will signal your body that it is preparing for bed.

3. **Avoid Nicotine.** Nicotine, the chemical found in cigarettes and other tobacco products, is a stimulant, and it makes it more difficult to fall asleep and stay asleep. Smokers also have interrupted sleep because they withdraw from nicotine during the night. This is the reason why so many smokers light up first thing in the morning.

4. **Avoid Alcohol.** Alcohol is a nervous system depressant, and many people are under the false assumption that it helps them fall asleep. Numerous studies have shown that alcohol use disrupts the normal brain wave architecture of sleep and leads to less restful sleep with more frequent awakenings. In short, alcohol will make you pass out, but it will not give you a good night's rest.

5. **Exercise.** While several studies have suggested that daily exercise improves sleep, a recent study reported by U.S. researchers in 2009 found that exercise might lead to less sleep. In general, it is best to avoid exercise within three hours of your bedtime. Falling asleep requires the body to lower its core temperature slightly, and exercise raises it.

6. **Use the bedroom for sleep and sex only.** Don't make your bedroom a multipurpose room. Keeping bedroom activities simple will prevent your body from getting conflicting signals.

7. **Keep Your Bedroom Cool, Dark, Quiet, and Comfortable.**

A few words of caution about prescription and nonprescription sleep aids: People with chronic insomnia have more pharmaceutical options than ever before to help them get to sleep. Many of them are safe and effective. However, these medications should be used only as a last resort. Some of the sleep drugs can be habit-forming, and all of them can have significant side effects. Make sure you discuss all your options thoroughly with your doctor, and under no circumstance should you self-medicate with over-the-counter painkillers, cough and cold medicines, illegal drugs, or alcohol.

THE #7 *EFFING PROBLEM: YOU ARE STRESSED OUT!

Stress is a normal neuropsychological reaction to a specific situation or event that generates feelings of worry, tension, or anxiety. The level of stress can vary widely from person to person, and it can vary considerably throughout your life. Stress can be acute, episodic, or chronic, and there are two primary sources: internal stressors and external stressors. Internal stressors usually arise from negative belief systems like toxic emotionality, low self-esteem, negative self-talk, fear of success, fear of failure, and perfectionism. These nonsupportive mind-sets come from your subversive self and add stress to all aspects of life. External stressors come from the environment and include physical threats and extreme cold, heat, or pain. But fighting traffic, being overwhelmed at work, and having concerns about your marriage, kids, or finances are also good examples of external stressors. In most cases the anxiety caused by internal stressors compounds anxiety caused by the external stressors.

So why do you stress-out? Your body has a natural alarm system that warns you of danger and primes your muscles and internal organs for either escape or battle. This is more commonly called the "fight-or-flight" response. When a threat is recognized, the brain's hypothalamus releases chemicals that activate a portion of the nervous system called the sympathetic nervous system. Epinephrine (also called adrenaline) and norepinephrine flood the body, raising awareness, increasing your heart rate, tightening your muscles, and activating your sweat glands.

At the same time, cortisol is also released. This so-called "stress hormone" provides an immediate boost of energy for your brain and muscles by increasing sugar levels in your bloodstream. The stress response is triggered almost instantaneously by both real and perceived threats. Even emotional conflicts can trigger the stress response, because the brain's emotional center, known as the limbic system, has direct connections to the hypothalamus.

In the prehistoric past, the stress response helped your ancestors escape from predators, protect their resources, defend their young, and survive natural disasters like fires or floods. Whenever and wherever these kinds of threats occur today, the stress response still plays this important lifesaving role. But the advancement of civilization has created different kinds of stressors that are not effectively managed by the crude fight-or-flight response. These are the stressors of modern-day life: finances, love, children, illness, divorce, and powerlessness. These stressors are thought to result in a persistent low-level activation of the fight-or-flight response, and over time this can have a devastating effect on your body.

The Stress Test

How stressed-out are you? Take this simple stress test. Give yourself one point for each "yes" answer.

1. Do you worry a lot, especially about things you cannot control?
2. Have you been sleeping too much or too little lately?
3. Have you been having abrupt mood changes?
4. Have you developed new physical problems like diarrhea, constipation, headaches, or body aches?
5. Do you rely on comfort foods, alcohol, cigarettes, or drugs to "settle your nerves"?
6. Are you feeling overwhelmed and having difficulty concentrating?
7. Are you increasingly restless, biting your nails, or grinding your teeth?

If you answered yes to any of these questions, there is a good chance your stress levels are too high!

If stress is not managed effectively, it begins to cause problems inside your body. By raising sugar levels in the bloodstream, the stress hormone cortisol alters how the body metabolizes fat and sugar, significantly raising the risk of obesity and type 2 diabetes. In response to stress, the brain and nervous system also release a chemical known as neuropeptide Y (NPY). It is believed that NPY can "unlock" receptors on fat cells, making them multiply and grow larger. Excess stress is perhaps the most common cause of overeating, which only compounds the problem.

The increased level of cortisol also impairs the immune system, making stressed-out people more prone to coughs, colds, flu viruses, and other infectious diseases. For the same reason, stress is thought to worsen autoimmune diseases like rheumatoid arthritis, lupus, and multiple sclerosis. Excess stress may even raise the risk of some cancers, because the immune system is thought to play an important role in cancer prevention. In fact, one study conducted by Swedish researchers found that women who were under a lot of stress were twice as likely to develop breast cancer, and other studies have found that stress hormones can fuel the growth and spread of cancerous tumors. Stress is, of course, a common cause of anxiety and depression. It can cause menstrual disorders in women, erectile dysfunction in men, and sexual dysfunction in both sexes. Stress has also been linked to ulcers, chronic constipation and diarrhea, gum disease, high blood pressure, and possibly stroke.

What stressful life events are most likely to raise the risk of illness? According to the Holmes and Rahe Stress Scale, the death of a spouse raises the risk of illness the most. Divorce, marital separation, imprisonment, and the death of a close relative complete the top five stress-induced health hazards.

The *Effing Solution:
The Chill Factor

True *Effing Fact

The Broken Heart Syndrome

Doctors at Johns Hopkins University used sophisticated heart tests and found that the surge in adrenaline from one tragic or shocking event can cause a sudden decrease in the heart's pumping capacity. The study was published in the *New England Journal of Medicine*. This "broken heart syndrome" is technically referred to as stress cardiomyopathy.

While most people easily recognize acute stress and episodic stress, chronic stress often goes unrecognized. The symptoms of chronic stress can be subtle: weight gain, mood swings, difficulty concentrating, changes in sleep, and headaches are common and often dismissed. It's believed that this unrecognized and undertreated chronic stress is the most dangerous to our health.

It is not possible to eliminate stress altogether, but just about anyone can learn how to better manage their stress by following a few simple steps.

Exercise. Chronic stress results from the persistent and inappropriate activation of your fight-or-flight response. Since your body is primed for battle or escape, physical activity is an ideal way to relieve the tension. Exercise does place significant stress on the body, and in the short term, exercise increases levels of the stress hormone cortisol. But over time regular exercise causes resting cortisol levels to drop, and this helps reduce stress. Plus, exercise causes the release of neurotransmitters known to improve mood, and it helps the body produce natural painkillers called endorphins.

Common Signs of Chronic Stress
Mental fogginess or memory problems
Irritability and/or moodiness
Headaches
Backaches
Muscle tension
Sleep disturbances
Weight changes
Fatigue

Take charge. Control what you can. Troubling events are most stressful when there is a lack of control over the circumstances or a perceived lack of control. That's why it is extremely important to take charge of your stress and control what you can. For instance, suppose you are stressed about losing your job in the next round of corporate layoffs. Because these kinds of personnel cuts are often impersonal bottom-line decisions, you have little control over the circumstances. While you may not be able to save your job, you can save your money—and you should. By exerting control over your spending and your savings, you will improve your financial situation in the event of an actual layoff and minimize the stress caused by a potential layoff. You can also explore other career opportunities, prepare a résumé, or learn a new skill. Remember, controlling what you can is the most important step in controlling your stress.

Take a Break. Once you identify the person or circumstance causing most of your stress, it is a good idea to lower your exposure. Being constantly confronted by a stressor magnifies the stress, making problems seem larger and more intimidating. It's like being at the foot of a mountain. But when examined from a distance, even Mount Everest seems less daunting. Taking a step back from your problems makes them appear more manageable and less stressful. When you are stressed, sidetrack yourself with productive and positive actions.

Take a Nap. Sleep and stress are closely connected. The lack of sleep is well known to increase stress levels, and high stress levels make it much more difficult to get a good night's sleep. Sleep deprivation increases the release of cortisol in the body, and those higher levels persist for longer periods of time. There is also some evidence to suggest that you become more sensitive to stress hormones as you age, which is one reason why most people "sleep like babies" until middle age. According to the Better Sleep Council, more than half of all Americans say stress disturbs their sleep, and 36 percent say stress keeps them awake at night at least once a week. Getting adequate amounts of sleep is essential to good emotional and physical health. Making sleep a priority will help you manage your stress more effectively.

Rub it out. Getting pampered at the spa is a luxury few people can afford, but massages can be very therapeutic, and they are one of the most effective relievers of stress. According to a 2006 survey conducted by the American Massage Therapy Association, more than one in six U.S. adults have had at least one massage. Massage increases the release of endorphins, natural chemicals known to relieve pain, relax muscles, and improve mood. Physical touch is also a basic human need, and the close human contact of a massage may help improve self-esteem.

Massage therapy can loosen tight shoulders, alleviate headaches, improve back and neck pain, and relieve anxiety.

There is also some evidence to suggest that massage can lower blood pressure, improve circulation, improve sleep, and boost immune system functioning. The American Massage Therapy Association provides a list of qualified massage therapists. If you are concerned about the cost, therapeutic massage is sometimes covered by health insurance plans, and massage therapy schools often offer discount rates. There are also self-massage techniques that can relieve stress.

For self-massage tips and techniques from WebMD visit the website:

http://www.webmd.com/balance/stress-management/features/massage-therapy-stress-relief-much-more.

For video of self-massage techniques visit this website at eHow.com:

http://www.ehow.com/videos-on_3998_do-therapeutic-self-massage.html.

Tune in and tune out. Music can have a profound impact on your emotions, although the reason for this is not entirely clear. Canadian researchers recently discovered that emotionally charged songs cause the release of dopamine in the pleasure centers of the brain. This is the same area stimulated by drugs in drug addicts. Maybe that is why you feel chills down your spine when you hear certain songs, or why you emotionally

True *Effing Fact

Massage therapy is the most common form of alternative or complementary medicine used in U.S. hospitals.

relate to certain lyrics. Some studies have suggested that classical music or contemporary tunes that are slow and quiet are the most effective stress reducers, but other studies have found that all types of music reduce stress. In clinical trials music therapy has been shown to reduce preoperative anxiety and postoperative pain. In 2009 a review of twenty-three previously published studies found that listening to music lowered blood pressure, heart rate, and levels of anxiety in heart patients. And several studies have found listening to music improves mood and reduces chronic pain. For extra tips on the stress-relieving power of music, visit the American Music Therapy Association's website at www.musictherapy.org.

Smell the roses. Aromatherapy has been shown to help reduce stress levels in some scientific studies, but other studies have found no clear benefit. Proponents of aromatherapy say the scents emitted by essential oils and other plant compounds can help manage pain, lessen anxiety, relax mood, and improve concentration. Some claim that aromatherapy reduces stress because our sense of smell has a complex but direct association with the limbic system, the emotional center of the brain. Lemon scents, mango, lavender, and other fragrant plant oils are commonly used in aromatherapy for stress reduction.

Laugh a little. Laughter really may be the best medicine when it comes to stress reduction. Laughter has been shown to reduce the levels of stress hormones in the body, including cortisol, adrenaline (epinephrine), and noradrenaline (norepinephrine). It appears to work similarly to exercise, causing some chuckle enthusiasts to call laughter "exercise for your internal organs." Several studies have found that giggling can boost the immune system, improve sleep, relax muscles, improve blood flow, and lower blood pressure. A little bit of laughter has even been shown to help diabetics maintain healthy blood sugar levels. And as anyone who has ever hit their thumb with a hammer can attest, laughing about the injury lessens the pain. Laughter triggers the release of pain-relieving endorphins. Plus, psychologists say a hearty laugh provides an important emotional release.

Few Die Laughing

Infants as young as seventeen days old have been shown to laugh. Children laugh roughly 400 times a day, while adults laugh just 16–20. Some researchers claim that having a good sense of humor can add eight years onto your life. Unfortunately, our sense of humor declines as we get older, and that is no laughing matter!

Meditation. Meditation is often dismissed as New Age nonsense, but numerous scientific studies have proven that meditation is a very effective weapon for managing stress. Meditation calms the mind, slows breathing, improves oxygenation, and lowers levels of cortisol in the body. Studies have shown that older people who meditate live longer, have better brain function, have reduced blood pressure, and have a significantly lower risk of dying from cancer or heart attack. Older people who meditate also feel less old. There are many different kinds of meditation, and the skills have to be taught properly and then practiced. But once you get the hang of it, meditation can be a powerful and cost-free way to break free from stress.

Here are some behaviors you should avoid to lower stress levels:

- *Don't* overschedule your life. Make time for loved ones and activities you enjoy.

- *Don't* treat your stress by self-medicating with sleeping pills, alcohol, cigarettes, or drugs.

- *Don't* overeat comfort foods to cope with your stress.

- *Don't* react to stressful situations in violent or impulsive ways.

- *Don't* bottle up your stress. Talk about your stress to your family and close friends or speak to a mental health professional.

THE #8 *EFFING PROBLEM: YOU'RE NOT WASHING YOUR HANDS

Get ready to be grossed out. More than 90 percent of people say they wash their hands after using the bathroom, but studies have shown that just 83 percent of people do. Other studies have found that only 75 percent of women and 51 percent of men wash their hands after using the toilet, and the average hand-washing time was a hurried eleven seconds. Teenagers and children wash their hands even less frequently than adults, and when they do wash, they often do not use soap. Only 30 percent of people wash their hands after sneezing or coughing into them. Many people don't wash their hands before or after meals, while preparing food, or after playing with their dogs or cats.

We touch doorknobs, pick through dirty laundry, shake hands, high-five, and fist-bump one another, and scratch ourselves in unusual places—all without giving our hands a good scrub. As a result our hands are teeming with millions of germs, and we are constantly swapping them with those around us. Researchers at the University of Colorado used sophisticated gene sequencing and found that the average palm surface is home to more than 150 different species of bacteria. Yuck! The same researchers found the left hand and the right hand can have dramatically different populations of bacteria, and although women are more consistent hand washers, female hands have significantly more germs.

Hundreds of millions of people will catch colds this year, and roughly 30 million will come down with the flu. While nobody dies from the common cold, it is the leading cause of missed school days and missed work. The flu, on the other hand, is a much more serious illness. Influenza infections are responsible for at least 150,000 hospitalizations each year and 30,000–40,000 deaths. Pandemic flu strains, like H1N1 or mutated avian influenza viruses, have the capacity to kill millions. Most of us catch these viruses by shaking hands with a sick person or touching surfaces they have contaminated. Many of these infections could be prevented by consistent and proper hand washing.

Improper hand hygiene is also a common source of food poisoning, and each year 76 million Americans contract illnesses due to contaminated food. Touch is also the primary means of transmission of the drug-resistant superbacteria MRSA. In fact, roughly 80 percent of all infectious diseases can be transmitted by touch, and that is why the CDC and the World Health

True *Effing Fact

Hand-to-Hand Combat

Studies have shown that hand washing with soap:

- Cuts the risk of contracting a diarrheal illness nearly in half.
- Reduces pneumonia and other respiratory tract infections by 25–50 percent.
- Can reduce school absences by 50 percent if performed at least four times per day.
- May be more effective than drugs at preventing the spread of the SARS virus, bird flu, the H1N1 swine flu, and other flu viruses.
- May be more effective at controlling the spread of superbacteria (such as MRSA) in hospitals than isolating infected patients.
- Reduces the risk of skin diseases, intestinal worms, and eye infections.

Organization (WHO) recommend hand washing as the single most effective measure against catching sickening germs.

The *Effing Solution: Become a Soaper Hero!

Simply using soap and water is effective enough to substantially reduce the risk of infection. Antibacterial soaps may offer some added protection, but the research is far from convincing. Additionally, there is some concern that the use of antibacterial soaps is contributing to the emergence of multiple drug-resistant strains of bacteria. Alcohol-based sanitizing gels are very effective for cleansing the hands, and they are especially useful if there is no soap and water available. Most people don't know when or how to properly wash and dry their hands, but by following a few simple steps, just about anyone can become a "soaper hero."

How to Become a "Soaper Hero"

When to wash . . .

1. Before and after preparing or eating food.
2. After using the bathroom.
3. After touching pets or other animals.
4. After working or playing outdoors.
5. After sneezing or coughing into your hands.
6. After visiting or contacting sick relatives or friends.
7. Before and after changing your contact lenses.
8. After changing the diapers of a baby or young child.

9. After handling garbage.

10. Before and after treating a wound.

How to wash . . .

1. Use clean, running water.
2. The water should be warm, not hot or cold.
3. Scrub vigorously to a lather for at least twenty seconds. This is about the time it takes to sing "Happy Birthday" two times.
4. Make sure you wash the back of the hands, the wrists, between fingers, and around fingernails.
5. Rinse hands thoroughly under the running water, occasionally rubbing hands together.
6. Dry your hands thoroughly.*
7. Turn faucet off with a towel.

*Studies have shown that most people stop drying their hands when they are only 50 percent dry—especially if they are using an air drier. Wet hands are about a thousand times more efficient at growing and transmitting bacteria, so make sure they are adequately dry. Even drying them on your clothes is better than not drying them at all.

THE #9 *EFFING PROBLEM:
YOU'RE A JUNK FOOD JUNKIE

Today the average American has more dietary choices than ever before. But with longer work hours, less family time, and cheap convenient food on nearly every street corner, many of us are making the wrong choices. The United States is the world's top consumer of fast food, spending 1.46 billion dollars each year— or about five hundred dollars per person. No other country comes close to that amount. Americans eat one hundred acres of pizza each day—that's 350 slices eaten every second and 3 billion pizzas each year. Each year we also chow down 5 billion hamburgers with 2 billion side orders of french fries, and wash them down with billions of sugary sodas and several million milkshakes. We have breakfast at buffets, Chinese takeout for lunch, and Mexican drive-through for dinner. We munch on salty snacks between meals and almost always save room for dessert. Each year more than 47 million Twinkies are eaten in the United States, along with countless doughnuts, cupcakes, cookies, ice cream, and sugary treats. These kinds of foods and drinks are fine as occasional indulgences, but unfortunately they have become staples of the Western diet.

It *Effing Figures

Where's the Beef?

There is surprisingly little meat in the average fast-food hamburger. Researchers from the Cleveland Clinic in Ohio tested eight popular brands of hamburger and found that the average burger was just 12 percent meat. About half of the burger weight was water. The same group of researchers previously found that hotdogs contain less than 10 percent meat.

So why are we eating so much bad stuff? The first reason, which is perhaps the most important reason, is because we can. Prosperous nations with more food choices get fatter. It's that simple. We want it, we buy it, we eat it, and then we pay a high price for it later in poor health. Several studies have shown that as the number and variety of food choices increases, so does the amount of total calories consumed. Variety is not the spice of life; rather, it is the vice of life. Having lots of choices is making us fatter. The number of items in a typical U.S. supermarket has tripled since 1980, and during this same time period there has been a rapid rise in overweight and obesity. It is probably not a coincidence. Today there are nearly fifty thousand products on the shelves at your average supermarket. Most Americans are eating too much—and eating the wrong stuff.

The second reason for our national eating disorder is more compelling, and it certainly grabs more headlines: fast food and junk food may be mildly addictive. Access to adequate nutrition really didn't improve significantly in Western cultures until modern times, and in some parts of the world, food scarcity is still an alarming problem. So in evolutionary terms, fast foods and junk foods are brand-new developments. Your prehistoric ancestors had to work much harder for their food than you do today, and there was much less food to go around. It was during this difficult time period—at least hundreds of thousands of years ago— that your uncontrollable appetite for junk food and fast food probably took root. Foods high in fat, salt, or sugar are exceedingly rare in nature. But these kinds of meals are high in energy. All the calories and the fat, salt, and sugar helped your ancestors survive. So the human body and brain evolved to seek out these high-energy meals.

But now this biological survival mechanism is believed to be backfiring, creating cravings for bad food in a time of nutritional abundance. Though it is still very controversial, evidence is mounting for the addiction hypothesis. Foods that are high in fat and sugar are known to increase the release of pleasure chemicals inside the brain and stimulate the brain's pleasure center. In fact, the brain's response to fats and sugars looks a lot like the effect of heroin or nicotine, albeit to a lesser degree. Overeaters prefer junk food and exhibit many of the compulsive and destructive behaviors seen in drug addicts. Junk food also causes the blood sugar to peak and then plummet, causing a strong desire for another sugar fix. Some experts believe that food additives like monosodium glutamate (MSG) can be addictive, and animal studies suggest that bingeing on foods that are high in fat, sugar, and salt may even cause permanent changes in brain structure.

So how dangerous are these diets? Eating high amounts of junk food has been linked to obesity, type 2 diabetes, and an increased risk of heart disease, heart attack, and stroke. The large amounts of fat and salt found in many junk foods also increases the risk of hypertension, high cholesterol, thyroid disease, dementia, kidney disease, fatty liver, and several types of cancer.

Signs YOU Might Be a Junk Food Junkie

1. You fantasize about eating junk food.
2. Your junk food habit has affected your health.
3. People have criticized you for the amount of junk food you eat.
4. You frequently feel guilty about your diet.
5. You get a pleasurable rush after eating junk food.
6. Over time you have been eating more and more junk food.

7. You hide your junk food habit.

8. You eat junk food or fast food every day.

THE *EFFING SOLUTION: BREAK THE JUNK FOOD HABIT

There have been some positive changes in the food industry. Most large fast-food chain restaurants offer healthier low-calorie alternatives, and some restaurants have completely eliminated artery-clogging trans fat from their menu items. Improved food-labeling laws have made it easier to identify healthy foods at the supermarket, and some cereal companies are no longer marketing sugary cereals to children. But most snacks, prepared foods, fast foods, and meals sold at your favorite restaurants are still loaded with calories, fat, salt, and sugar. Don't rely on the food industry. If you're a junk food junkie, you must break the junk food habit on your own.

Step 1: Reality Check

Most people who say, "I'm starving" are not in fact starving. Many of them are not even hungry. In other parts of the world, men, women, and children are indeed starving. The average American has enough fat stored in their hips, bellies, and thighs to last a week without eating any food whatsoever. So lose the theatrics. You are not going to die of starvation by eating less or skipping a meal every once in a while. You eat mostly out of routine—not hunger—and so do most Americans. As a result we have become a nation of conditioned overeaters. Habitual overeating is not a problem if you are eating healthy foods, but most of us are not. So it is essential that you eat only when you are truly hungry and stop when you are no longer hungry. Never eat until you feel full! It takes about twenty minutes for your stomach to signal your brain that it has had enough food. If you are eating to the point of feeling full, you are eating way too much.

Step 2: Examine Meal Motivation

During times of emotional strain you are primed to make poor dietary decisions. When you feel blue or stressed, your brain craves a bad food fix. So you feed these feelings instead of your appetite with comfort foods, snacks, and desserts. Studies have shown that junk foods flood your brain's pleasure center with dopamine, the satisfying "reward" neurotransmitter, and mood-boosting endorphins. This makes you feel good, but only for a little while. The high is followed by a crash and more cravings.

Over time these junk foods increase your daily stresses and prompt more poor food choices. This vicious cycle is just one of the many reasons why people suffering with major depression or anxiety have an increased risk of being overweight and obese. If left unaddressed, feelings of anger, frustration, boredom, or sadness can trigger a similar kind of emotional eating in most people. You are not alone. So it is important to learn how to talk about your feelings instead of swallowing them with a bag of chips. If necessary, speak with a licensed psychologist about developing more effective coping strategies.

But there are some other important motivators for bad food choices. Food is often used as a distraction or a means of procrastination, or sometimes people just eat out of greed. Before you head to the drive-through, snack machine, doughnut shop, or pizza parlor, it is critical to ask yourself, "Why do I want to eat right now?" If you are truly hungry, then eat something—but eat something nutritious.

Step 3: Make Convenience Food Inconvenient

There are more than 11,000 Burger King restaurants in the world today and more than 31,000 McDonald's restaurants. Yum! Brands, Inc., the parent company of Pizza Hut, Taco Bell, and Kentucky Fried Chicken (KFC) is the world's largest restaurant company, operating 34,000 food service facilities in one hundred countries. There are roughly 145,000 convenience stores and 69,000 pizza parlors in the United States alone. Fast food and convenience items are hard to avoid, so you have to take steps to make these options less convenient.

Making Convenient Inconvenient

1. Don't carry cash. Eighty percent of purchases at fast-food restaurants are still made with cash. If you don't carry cash, you're less likely to purchase fast food or convenience foods.
2. Carpool to work. No car, no drive-through.

3. Brown-bag your lunch. Bringing lunch makes dining out or takeout less convenient. Plus, most people resist throwing out food they have brought to work.
4. Take highways or residential roads that are not lined with tempting restaurants.
5. Shop for the week at the supermarket.
6. Keep snack foods and desserts out of sight at home.
7. Brewing coffee at home may stop you from buying a dough-nut, muffin, or other treat at the local coffee shop.

Step 4: Make Healthy Foods More Convenient

In addition to making junk foods less convenient, it is important to make healthy foods more convenient. Keep bowls of fresh fruit around the house and fresh vegetables in the refrigerator. Place healthy, low-calorie snacks in baggies and bring them to work with you. Or better yet, bring an apple. Most of your meals should be home-cooked. Foods cooked at home usually have lower amounts of salt, fat, and sugar. Buy containers so you can take the homemade leftovers to work. These steps often save you time and money. Plus, significantly improving your diet may even save your life.

Step 5: Retrain Your Taste Buds

The human taste buds detect five basic tastes: sweet, sour, salty, bitter, and umami. Umami is the newest addition to our understanding of taste, and it comes from the Japanese word for "tasty" or "savory." Foods with strong umami include meat, cheeses, and mushrooms. Genetics play a large role in determining our ability to taste, but the way we develop a preference for specific foods is through taste exposure. And let's face it, a lot of healthy foods are not inherently tasty. They just don't pack the same kick as high-fat, high-salt, and high-sugar junk foods.

But you can develop a *distaste* for salty, fatty, and sugary foods. Just ask anyone who has switched from sugared cola to diet cola. After a short time the sugared cola tastes too sweet to them. Try to eliminate aggressively flavored junk foods from your diet—like nacho chips, desserts, pizza, and candy. Then slowly introduce healthier unprocessed foods. Chew your food well and savor each bite, and you will begin to detect the subtle flavors found in many health foods. Mix blander foods like beans with spices and more savory health foods. If the texture of foods like seafood, tofu, or mushrooms turns you off, try mixing them with foods that have a more pleasing texture, like whole wheat pastas and breads. You will feel much better, and before long, your old junk diet choices will seem too salty, fatty, or sweet.

Step 6: Become a Perimeter Shopper

Next time you are in the supermarket, notice how the foods are arranged. In most supermarkets the natural and more healthful foods can be found along the perimeter, while most junk foods and processed foods are found in the aisles. Limit *most* of your shopping to the perimeter of the supermarket—this is usually where you will find the dairy, fresh fruits, vegetables, meats, and seafood.

Step 7: Stay Busy

Boredom is one of the most common causes of snacking and overeating.

Step 8: Stay Hydrated

Drink before you eat. Sometimes thirst is mistaken for hunger, and having a glass of water or a low-sugar juice may reduce some of the cravings for food. But never hydrate with sugary sodas. Each twenty-ounce bottle of this liquid candy has the equivalent of fifteen teaspoons of sugar, and each twelve-ounce can has ten teaspoon equivalents. In a typical year, the average American will drink fifty-six gallons of soft drinks, or just about six hundred twelve-ounce cans! A 2007 study from Yale University researchers found that people who drink soda eat more food calories, too. Remember to hydrate, but hydrate healthy.

THE #10 *EFFING PROBLEM: YOUR DOCTOR AND YOUR MEDICINES

Health professionals are imperfect. All doctors and nurses make mistakes, and some of them make a lot of mistakes. Though the numbers are often disputed, the Institute of Medicine claims that as many as 98,000 people die unnecessarily each year in the U.S. due to medical errors. How does this compare to other well-known killers? Motor vehicle accidents kill only half that amount—roughly 43,000 people each year. Breast cancer kills 42,000, and AIDS kills approximately 17,000.

Medical mistakes are a serious health hazard, and each year they could be killing more Americans than AIDS, breast cancer, and traffic accidents combined. On top of that, medical mistakes injure another 1.5 million people annually. Of course, the healthcare industry saves countless lives, but in doctor offices, clinics, and hospitals across the country, patients are misdiagnosed, harmed by prescription drugs, or maimed in hospital operating rooms with alarming frequency.

The U.S. is also the most medicated nation on Earth, and that is a big part of the problem. More than half of all Americans are currently taking at least one prescription medication, and one in six are taking three or more drugs, according to statistics from the Department of Health and Human Services (HHS). Almost half of the elderly take three or more prescription medicines. Antidepressants are the most commonly prescribed drug in the United States according to the CDC, with more than 164 million prescriptions

It *Effing Figures

Depression Drugs Double in Decade

A 2009 report from researchers at Columbia University and the University of Pennsylvania found the number of people taking antidepressant medication doubled between 1996 to 2005, from 13 million people to 27 million.

written in 2008 alone. That is depressing. Over the past two decades the use of prescription drugs has skyrocketed, and now more than 3.5 billion prescriptions are filled each year. Due to increased availability, clever marketing campaigns, and ethically questionable drug industry influence, doctors are more likely to prescribe drugs than ever before.

Most of the drugs in use today, even for serious conditions like heart disease and diabetes, have never been tested rigorously in combination with other common drugs. Yet millions of Americans are taking multiple prescription drugs with little evidence that a combination will be effective. These prescription drugs are often mixed with vitamins, over-the-counter remedies, or herbal medicines, which compound the risks. Many times these prescription medicines are used with alcohol or illegal drugs, which can dramatically reduce medication potency or increase toxicity. Doctors and pharmacists are on the lookout for potentially dangerous interactions, but the system is far from foolproof. All drugs can have significant side effects, and the chances of having a significant side effect increases with each drug you take. When it comes to taking medicine, sometimes less is more.

THE *EFFING SOLUTION: CONTROL YOUR CARE

Don't be laissez-faire and uninformed about your healthcare. If you are like most Americans, you probably have no problem questioning your auto mechanic, but you rarely question your doctor. Good healthcare is so much more important than good car care, and you must start giving your health the high priority it deserves. To reduce your risk of being a victim of medical mistakes, you have to first take control of your care. Here are some simple but very effective measures you can take to dramatically reduce the risk of medical errors:

1. **At home:** Have a list readily available with all of the medications you are currently taking, the doses, and the conditions being treated. On the list, write down which doctor ordered each prescription, the phone numbers for all your doctors, and all emergency contact information. The list should also include any allergies you suffer from or herbal supplements you are taking. Never use expired medications. If you smoke, stop smoking. If your doctor instructed you to stick to a special diet or lose some weight, give it an honest effort. We can tell when you haven't made the effort. Too often people rely on prescription medications to correct a health problem that could be more effectively managed with diet, exercise, and weight loss. This is especially true for type 2 diabetes, obesity, and high blood pressure.

2. **At the doctor's office:** Doctors' offices can be a hot spot for dangerous germs. Make sure your doctor and all other healthcare personnel wash their hands before they touch you. Don't be afraid to ask your doctors to remove their watches and clean their stethoscopes, both of which could be teeming with dangerous viruses and bacteria. If your doctor is ordering a diagnostic test, like a CT scan, x-ray,

nuclear scan, or MRI, ask them about the reason for the test and the potential risks and benefits. Ask your doctor about all medications being prescribed for you and the possibility of side effects. If the prescription is not electronic, make sure you can read the handwriting. All information about medications and diagnostic tests should be provided to you in language you can easily understand. Use an alcohol-based hand sanitizer to clean your own hands when leaving the office.

3. **At the pharmacy:** The pharmacist will usually provide you with printed information about your prescription medicine. Check this printed information with the information your doctor gave you. Speak to the pharmacist if there is a discrepancy. In fact, your pharmacist can help you if you have questions about any of your medications. Ask about side effects and potential interactions. Pharmacists are knowledgeable medical professionals who do much more than fill prescriptions. They are an integral part of your healthcare team. Your pharmacist can even contact your doctor.

4. **At the hospital:** Go to a hospital that is experienced in treating patients for your condition. Some studies have suggested that busier university-based hospitals may have better care and lower death rates. Again, make sure that all healthcare personnel wash their hands before they come in contact with you. Don't be afraid to ask hospital

staff to remove watches, clean stethoscopes, or tuck in ties. Learn the names of your doctors and nurses. Ask unfamiliar hospital personnel to identify themselves. Ask if infection control protocols and measures for medical error reduction are being taken by the hospital staff. Many times this information is provided when you are admitted to a hospital, or it may be posted in your room. Never allow a medication to be given to you without knowing what it is for. When discharged, ask for explicit instructions in terms you can easily understand. This should include information about prescription medications and their dosages, as well as any follow-up appointments. Some studies have suggested that your risk of dying in a hospital is increased if you are admitted on a weekend. But if you are experiencing a medical emergency, *don't wait* for Monday. Staffing at hospitals is typically lower during the weekend, but going to the hospital is still your best shot at survival.

Hospital Help

The U.S. Department of Health and Human Services maintains a website where you can find and compare the best-performing hospitals in your area (www.hospitalcompare.hhs.gov). HealthGrades offers a free state-by-state listing of hospital rankings on its website (www.health grades.com).

---

5. **Before an operation:** Make sure you completely understand the surgical procedure being performed and why it is being done. Ask about the benefits of a successful surgery and any possible risks. To prevent wrong-site surgery, mark the limb or body part to be operated on. The American Academy of Orthopedic Surgeons recommends that surgeons initial the limb or the part of the body being operated on. Ask your surgical team if they follow the "Universal Protocol" to prevent wrong-site surgeries, as defined by the Joint Commission. You can look this up at www.jointcommission.org. Discuss your medications, allergies, and medical history with your surgeon and your anesthesiologist.

Oops! In the Operating Room

Wrong-site surgery includes operations performed on the wrong side of the body, the wrong location, the wrong body part, or even the wrong person. While wrong-site surgery is a rare event, an estimated 5–10 cases are reported each day in the United States.

READER/CUSTOMER CARE SURVEY

We care about your opinions! Please take a moment to fill out our online Reader Survey at **http://survey.hcibooks.com**.

As a **"THANK YOU"** you will receive a **VALUABLE INSTANT COUPON** towards future book purchases
as well as a **SPECIAL GIFT** available only online! Or, you may mail this card back to us.

(PLEASE PRINT IN ALL CAPS)

First Name _____ MI. ___ Last Name _____

Address _____

State ___ Zip _____ City _____ Email _____

1. Gender
- ❑ Female ❑ Male

2. Age
- ❑ 8 or younger
- ❑ 9-12 ❑ 13-16
- ❑ 17-20 ❑ 21-30
- ❑ 31+

3. Did you receive this book as a gift?
- ❑ Yes ❑ No

4. Annual Household Income
- ❑ under $25,000
- ❑ $25,000 - $34,999
- ❑ $35,000 - $49,999
- ❑ $50,000 - $74,999
- ❑ over $75,000

5. What are the ages of the children living in your house?
- ❑ 0 - 14 ❑ 15+

6. Marital Status
- ❑ Single
- ❑ Married
- ❑ Divorced
- ❑ Widowed

7. How did you find out about the book?
(please choose one)
- ❑ Recommendation
- ❑ Store Display
- ❑ Online
- ❑ Catalog/Mailing
- ❑ Interview/Review

8. Where do you usually buy books?
(please choose one)
- ❑ Bookstore
- ❑ Online
- ❑ Book Club/Mail Order
- ❑ Price Club (Sam's Club, Costco's, etc.)
- ❑ Retail Store (Target, Wal-Mart, etc.)

9. What subject do you enjoy reading about the most?
(please choose one)
- ❑ Parenting/Family
- ❑ Relationships
- ❑ Recovery/Addictions
- ❑ Health/Nutrition
- ❑ Christianity
- ❑ Spirituality/Inspiration
- ❑ Business Self-help
- ❑ Women's Issues
- ❑ Sports

10. What attracts you most to a book?
(please choose one)
- ❑ Title
- ❑ Cover Design
- ❑ Author
- ❑ Content

TAPE IN MIDDLE; DO NOT STAPLE

BUSINESS REPLY MAIL

FIRST-CLASS MAIL   PERMIT NO 45   DEERFIELD BEACH, FL

POSTAGE WILL BE PAID BY ADDRESSEE

Health Communications, Inc.
3201 SW 15th Street
Deerfield Beach FL 33442-9875

FOLD HERE

Comments

2 Your *Effing Love Life

Zelmyra and Herbert Fisher met in elementary school and grew up together in the small but tight-knit community of James City, North Carolina. It is a place they still call home. When Herbert was nearly twenty years old, he asked beautiful, young, eighteen-year-old Zelmyra to marry him. She accepted. It was 1924, and at the time nobody suspected this would be a record-breaking romance. After all, he was Baptist, she was a Methodist, and they both took their faith seriously. The Fishers were also poor; they were African American, and tough times were getting tougher. Still, they made it work.

Several years ago, the Fishers earned a world record for having the longest marriage of any living couple, and on May 13, 2009, they celebrated their eighty-fifth wedding anniversary. Zelmyra, age 102, and Herbert, age 104, admitted to reporters that it wasn't always easy. Herbert worked hard as a mechanic at the local Coca-Cola bottling factory for more than three decades, and during the Great Depression he worked for as little as a nickel a day. Zelmyra worked for a little while, too. But the couple made saving money a top priority. Herbert built the family home in 1942, and the couple managed to put all five of their children through college. On Sundays Herbert and Zelmyra would attend different church services, and they still do. He likes watching baseball and golf. She doesn't. But they both enjoy watching television together and sitting on the porch and counting the cars on the trains that zip past their home. Neither Zelmyra nor Herbert has ever considered getting a divorce, and both say if they had to do it all over again, they would.

Marriage—they sure don't make it like they used to.

The significance of marriage as a social institution in the United States has been waning over the last few decades. According to the National Marriage Project at Rutgers University, there has been a 50 percent drop in new marriages since the 1970s. While the divorce rate has dipped over the last few decades, getting divorced is no longer as stigmatizing as it once was, and roughly 40 percent of all marriages are still destined for Splitsville. The likelihood of divorce for second and third marriages is even higher. Simply put, many people are making the wrong choice in life partners or they are giving up too easily.

True *Effing Fact

Divorce rates vary widely throughout the world. More than half of all marriages in Sweden end in divorce, but only 1 percent of marriages in India end in divorce.

Many people are also choosing to remain single longer. Unmarried adults are one of the fastest growing segments of the population, with roughly 101 million American singles today, according to the U.S. Census Bureau, and single women are out-pacing single men. This is creating unique conflicts about child-bearing and commitment. Couples are cohabitating with increasing frequency and often starting families without getting married. Today roughly 40 percent of all births in the United States are born to unwed parents, and slightly more than half of all households are headed up by singles.

Despite the changing love landscape, whether you want to get married or not, having a strong and committed relationship with another person can be emotionally and physically rewarding. The romantic partner is the single most important relationship for many people. Sharing your life with someone who makes you happy has been shown to reduce stress, lift depression, possibly lower the risk of dementia and heart attack, and might even make you live longer. So stop sabotaging your relationships and start connecting.

THE #1 *EFFING PROBLEM: FEAR OF COMMITMENT

Fear of commitment is most often a charge leveled at men who are reluctant to take a walk down the aisle, but recent evidence suggests that men and women fear commitment to the same degree. And it takes many forms. The truth is, committing fully to another person is a bit of a challenge for most people. Commitment takes time, and everybody is on a slightly different schedule.

But for some people, the time never arrives. For them, the fear of commitment is so overpowering, it interferes with all attempts at forming meaningful connections. They are often called "commitment phobes," and many of them are in deep denial. They usually claim to want a loving and lasting relationship, often blaming their lack of romantic success on poor timing or not having found the right person. Yet their string of failed relationships suggests an alternate explanation. They often have a long history of dysfunctional dating patterns, such as superficial hookups, serial monogamy, or pursuing unattainable partners. Do you recognize anyone in this list?

Common Types of Commitment Phobes

Cheater: Has affairs to destroy meaningful relationships.

Emotional Retentive: Keeps an emotional distance from their partners so the relationship can never evolve into a commitment.

Fling-a-Ling: Prefers one-night stands or brief relationships to remain unattached to any one partner.

Goose Chaser: Continues to pursue a partner who is unattainable or unavailable as a means of avoiding commitment.

Never Forever: Is racked with fear about the permanence of marriage.

Perfectionist: Faultfinder who is never completely content with a partner and delays commitment by waiting for Mr. or Miss Right.

Serial Monogamist: Forms many close relationships that seem to dissolve just when questions of commitment surface.

Because the fear of commitment is usually not limited to romantic life, you can spot a commitment phobe without dating them for years. The fear of commitment is a pervasive problem, affecting health, money, career, and other relationships. People with commitment phobia may change jobs frequently, avoid buying a home, or fail to complete college. They usually won't commit to a budget, a savings account, or a plan for retirement. They may allow close friendships to disintegrate for no obvious reason. They let health club memberships lapse and fail to keep doctor's appointments. And forget about making plans for a simple get-together! People with commitment phobia try to avoid all kinds of obligations to themselves and to others.

Commitment phobia in romantic relationships can be frustrating, and many wrongly assume it is caused by selfishness or egocentricity. As the alternate name suggests, the "fear of commitment" is first and foremost a *fear*. Very often it is an irrational fear. Many fear the permanence associated with being in a committed relationship—especially marriage—but other fears play an important role, too. Commitment may create fears of losing sexual variety, friends, or personal space and options. Fears about being responsibile or making a bad decision are also factors. The fear of failure sometimes underlies the fear of commitment, especially for those who witnessed a rocky relationship or ugly divorce when they were young. The good news is that overcoming fear is a lot easier than overcoming selfishness.

Fear of Commitment Gene?

Researchers at Sweden's Karolinska Institute discovered that men who carry a specific gene variation are less likely to be satisfied with their partners and less likely to commit. Men without any copies of the gene are more likely to be happy and devoted husbands.

THE *EFFING SOLUTION: COMMIT TO COMMITTING

Everyone has a different capacity for romantic commitment, which is determined by internal and external factors. Internal factors, like our genes, are fixed and only thought to play a small role in most cases of commitment phobia. On the other hand, external factors are variable and are thought to play a large role. These external factors are your life experiences and perceptions. Most often the fear of commitment is a learned response to your external factors, and like all learned responses, the fear of commitment can be unlearned.

What is Your Commitment Capacity?

Give yourself one point for each "yes" answer.

1. Can you make definite plans weeks in advance with friends?   ○ Yes ○ No

2. Have you dedicated yourself to a specific career or life path?   ○ Yes ○ No

3. Are you married, engaged, or in a relationship headed toward marriage?   ○ Yes ○ No

4. Do you share your worries and emotions easily with your partner?   ○ Yes ○ No

5. Is the happiness of your partner very important to you?   ○ Yes ○ No

A score of 3 or less suggests a low capacity for commitment. If you scored a 1 or 0, then you are probably a classic commitment phobe!

Step 1

Take a commitment inventory. Examine your life and analyze how committed you are to your romantic partner, job, career, family, and friends. Write down all of the areas in your life where you are NOT making a full commitment.

Step 2

Identify the fears. List all of the reasons why you are not making a commitment in these areas of your life. What scares you about committing to your partner, job, or family? You may notice that the fears that prevent commitment in romantic relationships are often the same fears that prevent commitment to family, friends, or career—such as the loss of options, the loss of personal time, and the fear of responsibility. But sometimes the fear of romantic commitment stands alone. Some may fear emotional commitment because they have been burned in previous relationships, or they fear marriage because divorce can exact a devastating financial toll. List all of your fears—be honest and thorough.

Step 3

Isolate your fears. Once you have listed all of your fears behind your commitment phobia, it is time to rank them in importance. Perhaps the loss of sexual variety is playing a large role in your fear of commitment, while the loss of personal space plays a much smaller role. Perhaps fear of failure is your biggest concern, because your parents went through a divorce and it caused a great amount of pain. Isolate all of these fears and rank them from the largest fear to the smallest.

Step 4

Communicate these fears. It is important to be honest with your partner. It might seem a bit uncomfortable at first, but if you cannot frankly discuss your fear of commitment with your partner, you will never be able to fully bond with each other. In a nonjudgmental setting, talk frankly about the issues you are having and see if you can develop any solutions.

Step 5

Negotiate and compromise. If the loss of personal time is your biggest issue, talk with your partner about having a weekly night out with friends. If the lack of personal space is the problem, perhaps you can turn one room into a personal retreat, such as a quiet study, an art studio, or a place for making crafts. A garage can become a gym or a work space. If the loss of sexual variety is the major concern, ask your partner to spice it up or try new things in the bedroom (tips on how to add more sizzle to your sex life will be discussed later in this chapter). If you fear failure in marriage, you may simply need more verbal reassurances from your partner that your bond is strong. If you fear the financial ramifications of divorce, discuss a prenuptial agreement. The objective is to find mutually satisfying solutions that will lessen or extinguish your fears.

Step 6

Start at the bottom. The fear of commitment is most often a combination of smaller, more manageable fears. But it is extremely difficult to tackle multiple fears at once, and fears at the bottom of your list are usually more easily solved than those at the top. So start at the bottom of your fear list and gradually work your way to the top. With time your overall fear of commitment will decrease, and you will become a lot more fulfilled *inside* the relationship. Once you have reached the top of the list, don't be surprised if you find yourself totally committed.

There are some other important points about the fear of commitment that deserve mentioning. Marriage does not cure the fear of commitment. Many commitment phobes marry for the wrong reasons. The fear of commitment inside a marriage may manifest itself as constant bickering, emotional blackmail, or repeated threats of divorce. Many people who remain in unhappy or abusive marriages also have a fear of commitment—to themselves. If you are not fully committed to your own well-being, you will never be able to commit to someone else. Being a doormat for another person is not a commitment of any kind.

If you love a person who has a fear of commitment, it is extremely important that you treat the problem as a fear, and one that can be addressed and overcome. The fear of commitment is an insecurity, not an insult. So try to resist nagging, guilt-tripping, or delivering ultimatums. And last, it is important to know when to walk away. Some people, even if they love each other, are just not meant to be together. If you cannot commit to your partner, or if your partner cannot commit to you, it might be time to walk away. But remember to leave with love. Leaving does not mean you have to stop loving.

THE #2 *EFFING PROBLEM: POOR COMMUNICATION

Good communication is essential to maintaining a healthy relationship, and the lack of communication remains a constant source of frustration for many couples. There seems to be an epidemic lack of understanding between the sexes. Often women say men don't listen and are emotionally detached, while men say women nag and complain a lot. All couples experience these kinds of communication problems from time to time. In fact, good communication is not a very natural process for anyone. For most people, whether you are in a relationship or not, good communication is a learned skill.

In the earliest phase of dating, the communication seems to flow freely. Your conversations are filled mostly with happy, seductive, and superficial banter. After all, you wouldn't think about starting a new relationship by telling a potential mate your deepest or most disturbing thoughts. During this early phase, you are guarded and less emotionally invested, and you portray yourself as being more likable and interested in your partner than you really are. Essentially, you are not your true self. Both you and your partner are like explorers discovering each other. These kinds of conversations become the dominant communication pattern inside your relationship, and it often sets the stage for communication problems later on. That doesn't mean you should start all relationships by revealing your darkest secrets. But with time there is very little left to discover about each other, and that can leave you feeling unfulfilled. Your relationship has fundamentally changed, and the pattern of communication must change along with it. Your communication strategy needs to be altered as your relationship evolves from discovery to devotion.

The ways men and women communicate share many similarities. But there are some clear differences in the ways men and women communicate, and these differences may be important contributors to the lack of understanding seen in many relationships. Talking about emotional issues raises stress levels in men, while it decreases stress levels in women. Women tend to use more emotional words and complex language while talking, texting, or sending e-mails, while men tend to be more direct and efficient in transferring information. One study found that women talk much more than men do, using three times as many words each day on average. However, more recent studies have suggested that both men and women chat to the same extent. And there may be a biological reason why men seem to have trouble hearing and understanding women. Brain imaging studies have revealed that male brains have a more difficult time interpreting female voices. A woman's voice is more complex and melodic than a man's voice, and men must recruit a part of the brain used for music interpretation to decipher female speech. For men, male voices require less brain power. Interestingly, the lack of complexity in the male voice may be the reason why both women and men with schizophrenia tend to hear hallucinations in male voices.

Communication is also deceptively complicated. There are two main methods of communication: nonverbal and verbal. Nonverbal communication includes actions, body language, facial expressions, tone of voice, and gestures. Nonverbal communication can also be symbolic, like sending flowers to a lover. Verbal communication is, of course, what we say and what we write. Most assume that verbal communication is the primary way we communicate with each other, but research suggests that the exact opposite is true. More than 90 percent of our face-to-face communication is nonverbal.

Communication Breakdown

Two famous studies conducted by psychologist Dr. Albert Mahrabian suggest that 93 percent of face-to-face communication between people was due to nonverbal cues. Here is the breakdown:

55 percent: Eye contact, body language, facial expression
38 percent: Tone of voice used
7 percent: Content of words used

Developing good communication skills is not a passive process. It requires actions and attention to detail. If you are having frequent misunderstandings, disagreements, or arguments with your significant other, it is time to act. The benefit of honing your communication skills transcends romantic relationships. It will help you on the job and on the street. And the good news is that just about anybody can become a better communicator by obeying the "Ten Commandments of Communication."

The *Effing Solution: The Ten Commandments of Communication

Before you sit down to "have a talk," it is important to be warned about the possibility of overcommunication. For some couples the problem is not the lack of communication but rather the presence of too much communication. When couples constantly talk about their "issues," their relationship becomes a runaway locomotive, pulling a load of emotions and resentments. Overcommunication will inevitably derail the relationship, and in some cases it leads to a full-blown train wreck. Want to get back on track? Stop talking about your problems.

Sometimes not talking about a problem is the best solution for both partners. When women are stressed-out, the cuddle hormone oxytocin is released in the brain and triggers a "tend and befriend" response. So stressed-out women reach out for help, seek comfort, and try to bond with others by sharing feelings. Oxytocin is secreted in the brains of stressed-out men too, but to a much lesser degree. For men the dominant reaction to emotional stress is the fight-or-flight response, which is governed by the hormone epinephrine. That's why when major issues arise in relationships, women want to talk but men want to walk.

So how can *not* talking help the situation for both sexes? Stress is relieved for women by venting their feelings. So if you are a man, just listen and allow her to vent. Resist offering advice unless directly asked for it. Most often women just want to be heard and understood, not helped. Being supportive and understanding, but saying very little, is often the most effective strategy. For men stress is most effectively relieved by either confrontation or escape. They are in fight-or-flight mode. Women should not press men for heat-of-the-moment conversations. Give men the time and space to de-stress before having any serious discussions. Women who do not allow their men's "flight" reaction to predominate will be inviting a "fight" reaction, and in many cases that leads to a nasty confrontation.

Ten Commandments of Communication

1. **Don't forget the positive:** Express both positive and negative emotions. Most often couples try to "communicate" only when something is wrong. Practice makes perfect, and you should be actively communicating what bothers you and what pleases you.
2. **Pick the right time and place:** Never have important conversations under the influence of drugs or alcohol. Choose a time and setting where both partners can be relaxed.
3. **Actively listen:** The goal of active listening is mutual understanding. Focus all of your attention on your partner when they are talking. Don't interrupt or plan a response. Listen attentively to show them you fully understand. Then repeat what was said and validate to them that you fully understand their concerns. Listen for the tone of voice used and watch body posture and facial gestures.
4. **Use your indoor voice:** Don't shout or scream.
5. **Tell the truth:** Remember, omissions are also lies.

6. **Use eye contact:** Make eye contact from time to time. It is a sign of respect, and it indicates that you are listening. Looking away appears dismissive or defensive.

7. **Say it, don't gray it:** Don't use innuendo or drop hints and expect your partner to catch on. Be direct and clear when expressing your feelings and needs.

8. **Check your body language:** In face-to-face communication, your body language actually says much more than the content of your words. So be careful with the messages you are sending with your facial expression, posture, and actions.

9. **Watch your words:** Don't forget to say "please," "thank you," "I love you," "I miss you," and "I understand." Never insult or personally attack, and avoid using absolute phrases like, "I never," "you always," and so on.

10. **What you say is not as important as how your words are interpreted.**

---

3 THE *EFFING PROBLEM: UNFAIR FIGHTING

Couples most frequently fight about money, work, sex, or the children. These issues are close to many people's hearts, and having intense yet opposite feelings from your partner is a normal part of any relationship. No two couples are alike. Some couples fight a lot while other couples fight very little. People have different temperaments; some have very long fuses, while others have very short ones. Even those with the highest argument thresholds can erupt under stressful circumstances.

Your cultural experiences also influence your tendency to bicker. Some cultures are a bit more reserved, while others are a bit more hotheaded. Your family dynamics and upbringing play an important role, too. But all couples fight from time to time. In fact, a complete lack of fighting in a relationship may be a troubling sign, suggesting hostility, apathy, or a lack of communication. The good news is that relationship satisfaction doesn't really depend on how much you fight or what you fight about. Psychological research suggests that *how* you fight with your partner is the critical factor.

Couples in loving relationships can fight and remain close if both

> ### True *Effing Fact
>
> A seventeen-year study of 192 couples found that couples who argue live longer than couples who do not argue.
>
> (*Source: Journal of Family Communication*)

partners are committed to fighting fairly. Conflicts do not have to be harmful or hurtful. If done correctly, conflict can actually be constructive, providing an opportunity to strengthen your relationship. In reaching a mutual understanding, you can build a deeper commitment to each other. Negotiating differences, reserving judgment, and attempting to resolve the issue at hand are the cornerstones of fair fighting. Unlike unfair confrontations, fair fighting lowers stress levels because it empowers and creates options for both partners. Some couples figure out how to fight fairly on their own, but others require some assistance.

Frequent, intense fighting is an unhealthy habit. Hostility increases heart risks for both partners, and it is usually a symptom of something larger. Perhaps there is a communication problem, some deep-seated resentment, or a loss of interest. Whatever the case, if you are constantly fighting with your partner, it is essential to explore what is lurking behind all the bickering and address the root problem. This usually requires the help of a skilled therapist. Otherwise, you are just treating the symptom and not the disease.

Deadly Silence?

Women who "self-silence," or fail to voice their opinion during a disagreement with their husbands, were four times more likely to die prematurely according to a study published in the *Journal of Psychosomatic Medicine*. Self-silencing had no effect on the mortality of men.

THE *EFFING SOLUTION: HOW TO FIGHT FAIR

When it comes to keeping the peace in relationships, the American poet Ogden Nash (1902–71) probably said it best:

> TO KEEP YOUR MARRIAGE BRIMMING,
>
> WITH LOVE IN THE WEDDING CUP,
>
> WHENEVER YOU'RE WRONG, ADMIT IT,
>
> WHENEVER YOU'RE RIGHT, SHUT UP.

Pick your battles. Not every transgression deserves a conversation, let alone an argument. Dismiss trivial matters and fight only about issues you are passionate about. Resist acting in the heat of the moment when emotions are high. Give yourself time to cool off, and then ask yourself if the issue is really worth creating a conflict over.

Allow time for apologies. Giving yourself some time can help you collect your thoughts and decide if the issue is worth fighting over, but it also gives your partner time to reflect on their actions. Don't deprive your partner of an opportunity to apologize. A heartfelt and unprovoked apology is one of the most sincere signs of commitment.

Pick the right time and place. Avoid arguing in front of others or in public places, and never argue in front of your children. Studies have shown that levels of the stress hormone cortisol are higher in young children whose parents exhibit a lot of verbal hostility toward each other. Frequent conflicts between parents may even interfere with the development of infants. Keep it private and keep it quiet.

Own your part of the problem. Avoid framing the problem as exclusively "his" or "hers" and instead frame it as "ours." There are two sides to every disagreement, and the onus is on you to accept responsibility for your share. Approaching a problem as a team will make your partner less defensive and more open to negotiation. Ask, "How can we make this work together?"

Be willing to compromise. Never enter an argument with non-negotiable demands. The objective of an argument is not to be proven right, but to reach an understanding. You must be willing to yield some ground to gain some ground.

Be honest and be kind. Edit yourself. Don't exaggerate, harshly criticize, or use insults. Both partners lose when an argument is based on falsehoods or when it degenerates into a personal attack. Insults are particularly damaging, and hurtful words are not easily forgotten. Repeat positive comments and avoid hurtful ones.

Stay focused on the present problem. Resist the urge to bring old issues into new arguments. If you throw the proverbial kitchen sink at your partner, he or she will feel attacked and become defensive. Your main concern will be lost in your other complaints. Stick to the present issue and keep your objective clear.

Sometimes winning is losing. Most people don't really care if they are right or wrong, but they want to be heard and they want to be understood. The goal of fair fighting is to reach a mutual understanding and a compromise. Once you have been understood, work on resolving the issue and ending the argument. If you insist on winning an argument and fighting until your partner is defeated, you will be creating a lot of resentment. If you want to see your partner defeated, there is probably a much bigger issue you are not addressing.

Don't involve third parties. Fight your own battles and don't bring other parties into your argument, especially children. This is a veiled attempt to gang up on your partner. It's a very unfair tactic, and it is rarely effective. Try to avoid statements like, "My mother says . . .," "My friend told me . . .," or "Everyone agrees . . ."

Don't speculate. Avoid putting words in your partner's mouth or speculating on your partner's motives. Instead, ask your partner directly.

Time-out. If tempers flare, take a time-out. Asking for a break is okay, just don't run away or emotionally retreat. Tell your partner that you intend to come back and revisit the issue, but you need some time to collect your thoughts.

Explore options. Present ways to solve the problem and ask your partner to provide his or her own solutions. Sometimes it is helpful to see how other couples have handled similar problems. The more options you create, the more likely the problem will be solved peaceably.

Don't let it drag on. Set a reasonable time limit for the argument and don't let it drag on. If you are still at an impasse after an hour of honest discussion, it might be time to agree to disagree, or just agree to revisit the issue at another time.

The end of the argument is the most important part. How you finish an argument is much more important than how it started. Both partners should feel comfortable with the outcome and secure in the relationship.

Maybe you *are* the problem. Before going on the offensive or becoming defensive, consider the possibility that your words or actions may actually be causing the problem.

Be open to saying you're sorry. People have a limited ability to argue but an enormous capacity to forgive. If you have hurt your partner in any way, apologize and ask for forgiveness.

The Five R's of Fair Fighting

Relax   Don't let your emotions rule.
Receive Actively listen to you partner.
Repeat   Repeat your partner's position.
Relate   Present your side of the issue.
Release Let it go.

Some couples are beyond repair and are locked into a cycle of hostility and resentment. Physical, verbal, or emotional abuse should never be tolerated under any circumstances. According to the Department of Justice, more than 1.3 million women and more than 835,000 men are assaulted by an intimate partner each year in the United States. If you are currently in an abusive relationship, the only advice you need is this: get help and get out. The National Domestic Violence Hotline offers free, anonymous, and confidential help for victims of domestic violence in all fifty states, twenty-four hours a day, seven days a week: 1-800-799-SAFE (7233).

THE #4 *EFFING PROBLEM: SEX

Sex is an important part of any romantic relationship. Making love is the most powerful way to express your physical and emotional bond with your partner. While many people believe that marriage brings an end to enjoyable sex, studies suggest the opposite is true. Couples in committed relationships have sex more frequently than singles, and they tend to be more satisfied with their sex lives. But many couples will still experience troubling sex issues at some point during their relationship. Mismatched sex drives, waning sexual desire, sexual dysfunction, stress, work, and raising children can strain a relationship to the breaking point.

The average American couple will have sex about fifty-eight times a year according to data collected by the General Social Survey. That's just about once a week. Couples under age thirty have sex about twice as frequently, while older couples tend to have sex much less often. Roughly 15 percent of couples have sex less than ten times a year. Some don't have sex at all.

Most Common Reasons for Not Having Sex

In a 2009 sex poll conducted by Consumer Reports National Research Center, eight in ten people said they avoided or delayed having sex with their partners in the past year. The five most common reasons for this are:

53 percent Too tired
49 percent Not feeling well, health issue
40 percent Not in the mood
30 percent Children or pets
30 percent Work

Men and women lead very different sex lives, and this often compounds the problem. Compared to women, men think about sex much more often, seek sex much more frequently, and rank sex higher in importance. Of course, some women have very high sex drives and some men have very low sex drives. But on average men have much stronger sex drives than women do. This is true for both heterosexuals and homosexuals. Studies have shown that gay men have sex more frequently than lesbians. The male sex drive peaks in the early twenties while the female sex drive peaks in the early to midthirties. The female sex drive is also much more dynamic. Unlike the male sex drive, which remains fairly consistent, a woman's libido ebbs and flows from day to day, and it can vary widely with hormonal fluctuations, cultural traditions, and environmental influences.

It's often said that a man's desire starts between his legs, while a woman's desire starts between her ears—and there may be some truth to it. Testosterone is the dominant hormonal force of sexual desire for *both* sexes. Men produce a lot of testosterone in their testicles, and women produce only small amounts in their ovaries. As a result, nonhormonal influences play a much larger role in creating female sexual desire. Women will often initiate sex to express intimacy, please their partner, improve their own well-being, or confirm their own desirability, while men are usually straightforward pleasure seekers. Sexual desire in women is complicated and not completely understood. In fact, most women don't even agree on what exactly turns them on.

Regardless of these differences, sex is an important expression of physical and emotional commitment for both men and women, and it is a very healthy habit. Studies have shown that sex can lower heart attack risk, reduce blood pressure, and lower stress levels. Having regular sex also lifts depression, improves self-esteem, relieves pain, and gives a boost to the immune system. Some studies have suggested that men who have a lot of sex have a lower risk of prostate can-

> *Sex is a lot like pizza.*
> *Even when it's bad,*
> *it is still pretty good.*
> —Anonymous

cer. Sex has also been shown to improve the sense of smell, relieve allergies, and help people fall asleep.

The *Effing Solution:
Seven Secrets of Seduction

Having good communication is essential for a healthy rela-tionship, and experts often recommend improving communi-cation as a means of improving your sex life. But good communication doesn't always translate into good sex. Many long-term couples communicate very well with each other but have unsatisfying sex lives. It is also possible to have great sex with someone you don't communicate well with. Sometimes you can have great sex with a virtual stranger. When it comes to having great sex, the importance of communication has been overemphasized. Instead, think back to when you first met your partner and recall the seduction. The real problem for many long-term couples is that they have simply forgotten how to seduce each other. By using the "Seven Surefire Secrets of Seduction," you can put the sizzle back in your sex life.

Seven Surefire Secrets of Seduction

1. **Tell your lover a sexy bedtime story.** Experts often say the brain is the most powerful sexual organ in the body, and one good way to engage it is with fantasy. So conjure up a story and share it with your lover at bedtime. It can be about a princess, a pirate, or a real person. Tell your lover how you want to be pleased or how you intend to please them. Just don't hold back! Getting graphic really gets the brain going.

2. **Say it before you do it.** Like professional athletes who visualize victories, the brain must be primed before the body can perform. It could be a breathy phone call at work, a naughty note left inside a purse or a briefcase, or just a racy text message. For some people the anticipation of sex can be nearly as rewarding as the act itself. So build anticipation and let the momentum take care of the rest.

3. **Bedtime is adult playtime.** There are plenty of toys and adult-themed games on the market, but sometimes it's better to get creative with the games you might already have around the house—plus, they're a lot more discreet. Try playing a few hands of strip poker, give naked Twister a spin, or just tickle your funny bone with a game of erotic Operation. Just roll the dice and use your imagination.

4. **Set the scene and look the part.** If you want an Oscar-worthy performance, set a scene that engages as many of the five senses as possible. Try some dim lighting, scented candles, delicious finger foods, wine, feathers, satin sheets, fluffy pillows, rose petals, or romantic music. Stimulate as many of the senses as you can. And don't forget to touch your lover often, even in nonsexual ways. Remember how you first seduced each other? Touching the arm, leg, or chest while chatting are strong signals of sexual interest. Touch is perhaps the most primal of the five senses, so use it often. Of course, make sure you shower, shave, and dress the part.

5. **Just do it.** Some sexologists call this the "Nike Philosophy." Even if it seems monotonous, experts say making love on a regular basis is critical to sustaining a healthy sexual relationship. Once couples stop having regular romps, it is often difficult to get back to previous levels of activity. It's like going to the gym; the hard part is getting there, but once you start sweating, it is always well worth the trouble.

6. **Have a naughty night out.** Forget date night! Instead, try a naughty night out. Maybe take your partner to a striptease, an adult toy store, a theme room at a motel, or even the backseat of your car. Pretend to meet in a bar and pick each other up all over again. Basically, if it feels like you are doing something wrong, you probably have the right idea.

7. **Novelty.** Break life's monotony by adding everyday novelty. The brain responds to novel situations with increased awareness and heightened senses. Feel-good chemicals like dopamine flood the brain when you change your routine or expose yourself to new situations, and dopamine is known to ignite romantic and sexual feelings in both sexes.

If you are experiencing any significant sexual issues in your relationship, it is extremely important to be evaluated for underlying medical and psychological conditions. Sometimes sexual dysfunction is a sign of a serious psychological or medical illness, and having all sexual problems assessed by a doctor is essential. Nonprescription and prescription medications are commonly overlooked as causes of sexual dysfunction or diminished sexual desire. If you started taking a medicine shortly before the sexual issues arose, they could be side effects of the medication. Talk with your doctor about switching to a different medicine.

Common Causes of Sexual Dysfunction or Loss of Sexual Desire

Psychological: Depression, anxiety, excessive stress, poor body image, and low self-esteem.

Medical: Heart disease, diabetes, hypertension, menopause, low testosterone, low thyroid, obesity, prostate cancer, enlarged prostate, back injuries, arthritis, and nerve damage.

Medications: Antidepressants, antianxiety drugs, high blood pressure medications, antihistamines, high cholesterol medications, nonsteroidal anti-inflammatory drugs (NSAIDs, over-the-counter pain relievers, such as aspirin and ibuprofen), prostate cancer medications, male pattern baldness medications, oral contraceptives, hormones, muscle relaxants, and drugs that treat gastric reflux.

Lack of sleep: A persistent lack of sleep decreases libido in both men and women, and increases the risk of erectile dysfunction for men.

Lifestyle factors: Smoking, excessive alcohol intake, alcoholism, drug abuse, and lack of exercise.

THE #5 *EFFING PROBLEM: YOU HAVE EMOTIONAL BAGGAGE

When romantic relationships fail, the brain is often forced to cope with a significant loss. Breakups can cause a loss of trust, security, a future, a friend, or a life partner. Escaping an unhealthy relationship may leave you with new fears or a devastated self-esteem. If the pain, fear, and loss of the breakup are not resolved immediately, our brains go on the defensive. Negative feelings are removed from our consciousness, and they are packed away inside subconscious suitcases. This compartmentalization allows us to function in everyday life, but we end up dragging this emotional baggage from relationship to relationship.

Unfortunately, emotional baggage doesn't only come from your romantic partners. Your early childhood experiences, family life, and interactions with friends and coworkers all shape your self-perception and your worldview. If you developed a lack of trust during childhood, you may be more guarded in adult relationships. If you have been betrayed by close friends, you may become suspicious of your lovers. The humiliation of losing a job may cause you to withdraw from a romantic partner. Any event that has an impact on your self-esteem is often stored as emotional baggage.

Do You Suffer from Post-Traumatic Dating Disorder?

In romantic relationships, emotional baggage creates what some call post-traumatic dating disorder (PTDD). Do you recognize the signs?

1. When your buttons are pushed, your emotions spill out.
2. You compare your new partner to previous partners.
3. You have erected emotional walls around yourself.
4. You always assume the worst in your current partner.
5. You constantly test your new partner.
6. Your actions do not match your words.
7. You often talk about your romantic past.

Most people do not recognize their own emotional baggage. If they do admit to carrying emotional baggage, they will often deny it is having a negative impact on their current relationship. Needless to say, both partners in a romantic relationship bring their own set of luggage, and sometimes it is difficult to sort out whose dirty laundry is creating the biggest stink. But if left unaddressed, emotional baggage will sabotage all attempts at forming stable relationships in the future.

THE *EFFING SOLUTION: CHECK YOUR BAGS!

Just like air travel, if you want your new relationship to take flight, you have to check your bags. To do that you must first pull the emotional baggage from the closet of your subconscious and bring it into consciousness where it can be dealt with. Then it's time to count how many bags you are carrying and exactly what you have packed inside them.

Take an inventory. On separate pieces of paper, write down all of your past relationships, and then list as many memories as possible for each. Include all the happy memories and hurtful moments. Then write down any dysfunctional lessons you might have learned from each relationship. Ask yourself, "How did this dating experience negatively shape my life?" Do this for all of your serious relationships. You might see a pattern evolve.

Create a real suitcase. Get a travel bag, a suitcase, or even a file folder and place your list of memories, lovers, and lessons learned inside of it. This will physically become your emotional baggage. Creating a physical home for your emotional baggage will help you deal with it in a more rational way.

Accept help with your bags. Once you have collected and analyzed your emotional baggage, open it up with your new partner or therapist. It is important to be honest, so make sure you do this in a nonjudgmental setting. Discuss your fears, past experiences, and how you think these events are shaping your present life. Ask for assistance from your partner or from your therapist to break these patterns. The following tips will get you started.

Bag Check!

1. Stop living in the past: avoid bringing up old relationships, memories, and events. Resist the urge to visit places where you used to go with your previous partner.
2. Shed your false confidence: admit that you have been hurt. Forgive yourself for being angry, sad, or depressed.
3. Accept vulnerability.
4. Stop comparing: don't compare your new partner or new relationship to previous ones.
5. Thought-block your obsessions: if you find yourself obsessing about someone from your past, redirect your mind or try to block the thought.
6. Focus on the "pleasant tense": concentrate on the present partner and all of the good things your current relationship offers.

Blame the relationship. Don't blame yourself or your past partner—blame the relationship. Sure, you might have made mistakes or even done a few bad things. Your partner may have done the same. But both partners played a role in the failure of the relationship. Accept the fact that some relationships are never meant to be. You don't have to forget, but you can forgive. Blaming the other person allows you to hold on to resentment.

Beware of people with matching luggage! You might be drawn to people who have a matching set of luggage, and that can be a combustible situation. It is often easy to bond with a partner who shares your pain, but the shared emotional baggage then becomes the cornerstone of your new relationship. Move into these relationships with extreme caution! If neither partner has effectively dealt with their emotional baggage, the relationship is doomed to fail. Other times you may search out those who are dragging a complementary set of luggage. For instance, a woman with father issues may choose a man who is domineering due to his own emotional baggage.

Close your suitcase. Once you have brought your emotional baggage out from the deepest recesses of your subconscious and discussed it openly, it is important to shut your suitcase. If old memories, patterns, or feelings resurface, remember that you have already given them a home. Put the issue back inside your suitcase where it belongs.

Get excited about a second chance. Novelty increases the release of dopamine, the pleasure neurotransmitter, inside the brain. So make powerful new memories for your new relationship. Go to different restaurants and hangouts. Take a vacation together. Act spontaneously and get creative.

The #6 *Effing Problem:
Relationshopping

You met a good man or a good woman, and at first things were exciting, new, and fun. But now you are not so sure. There is nothing really wrong with your current relationship, but you are bored and find yourself looking outside the relationship for a little excitement. Maybe you test the waters a little bit by flirting with the cute guy in sales or chatting with the pretty woman in marketing. You fantasize regularly about being with this other person, or perhaps being single again. You secretly tell your friends that you are keeping your options open. Sometimes you make a plan to stray, and if given the opportunity, you just might act on it.

If any of this sounds familiar, you have been "relationshopping." Relationshopping is also called the Grass is Greener Syndrome (GIGS), and it is very common. We are all born with an extraordinary, almost instinctual capacity to envy others and underappreciate our own circumstances. While people enjoy the predictability and stability of a relationship, they also bore easily. As a result, most couples in committed relationships will go through a phase where one or both partners will have serious doubts about the depth of their love interest. Some people are relationshopaholics, always looking to trade in their current partner or trade up to someone better.

It *Effing Figures

A survey of more than 35,000 women conducted by AOL Living and *Woman's Day* magazine found 52 percent of women did not think their husbands were their soul mates, and 72 percent of women have considered leaving their husbands.

The evidence that relationshopping is on the increase in the U.S. is overwhelming. Today people are less content to remain in long-term relationships, less likely to marry, and more likely to divorce than previous generations. Dating websites for people who are "married but looking" are popping up across the Internet, and divorced dads and cougars are prowling bars and boulevards in every neighborhood, looking for fresh meat.

Some experts believe that an overpowering fear of commitment may be the driving force behind relationshopping, but that is not likely the case. The fear of commitment is largely determined by past experiences, while relationshopping is based on the future or pure fantasy. Relationshopping is a form of dating speculation. It is a love gamble created by the fear that you may be settling for your current partner and you might be better off with someone else.

Another explanation for the Grass is Greener Syndrome is increased opportunity. People have more romantic options today than ever before—mingling with potential mates at work, at church, through friends, at parties, in nightclubs, and online. We know from diet studies that as the number of food options increases, appetite and the amount of calories eaten do as well. Love and sex are appetites, too, just like hunger. With so many sexual options, your love appetite may be in overdrive. You might even be a love glutton, always looking for a spicier or more satisfying dish.

THE *EFFING SOLUTION: RELATIONSHOPPING RECOVERY

Keep in mind that the overwhelming majority of relationships will fail. If you are thinking about leaving your current partner for another, you must accept the likelihood that the new relationship may not work out either. Sooner or later you will probably become ambivalent about the new partner, no matter how smoking hot or charming they may be. That is not being pessimistic; it's being realistic. Of course, some people "dump and jump" to a new partner and live happily ever after, but it is still unlikely.

If you are in a committed relationship and have been relation-shopping, it is important to ask yourself one critical question: if you started dating another person and it did not work out, would you still be better off? If your answer is "yes," then you must leave your current relationship. You will never be committed to your current partner, and you should not waste any more time. But if your answer is "no" or "I'm not sure," then your current relationship could be the one that lasts a lifetime, and all you may need is a little relationshopping recovery.

Relationshopping Recovery

- **Limit variety:** Stop creating and pursuing romantic options. By increasing your dating options, you are fueling the feelings of ambivalence and discontent in your current relationship. Stay away from bars, nightclubs, or places where available singles meet. Remember, the best way to avoid the Grass is Greener Syndrome is to stay far away from the fence.
- **Stop flirting with disaster:** Flirtation boosts self-esteem and makes us feel more desirable. But it also creates opportunities and fantasies that can be disastrous to your current relationship.

- **Stay off "Fantasy Island":** Recognize fantasy relationships for what they actually are—enticing but imaginary scenarios.
- **Focus on love, not lust:** Lust is a very powerful but very fleeting phase of any relationship. Lust never lasts forever. Concentrate on the other benefits of being in a loving relationship, such as trust, loyalty, intimacy, and friendship.
- **Keep it new:** Instead of allowing your ambivalence to trigger self-sabotaging behaviors in your relationship, recognize it as a signal that you need to spice things up. When presented with novel situations, the brain secretes the pleasure hormone dopamine. This is the same hormone that spikes in the brain when we first fall in love. Keep life interesting and do new things with your partner.
- **Water your own grass:** If you want your grass to be greener, you must water it and provide it with nutrients. Be trustworthy, kind, passionate, and compassionate with your partner and your grass will grow lush with love.

THE #7 *EFFING PROBLEM: INFIDELITY

Physical infidelity is the signal, the notice given,
that all fidelities are undermined.

—KATHERINE ANNE PORTER (1890–1980)

Statistics vary, but infidelity touches about half of all committed relationships. In 2007 MSNBC.com and iVillage.com reported results of their "Love, Lust, and Loyalty" online survey of more than seventy thousand adults. They found that one in five people in "monogamous" relationships admitted to cheating on their current partner. Taking the vow of marriage did not lower the risk of infidelity. In fact, the survey found that married couples cheated slightly more often—28 percent of married men admitted to cheating on their spouses as did 18 percent of married women. Twenty-seven percent of people who considered themselves "happily married" still strayed; so did 15 percent of married parents with young children. Separate studies conducted by researchers at the University of California in San Francisco and the University of Chicago found similar degrees of unfaithfulness.

True *Effing Fact

The Four-Year Itch?

Several studies have found that there is a gradual decrease in satisfaction over the first five years of marriage, and partners are most likely to cheat three to five years into a committed relationship. (*Source:* MSNBC.com)

There are several different kinds of infidelity. Physical infidelity can be opportunistic or obligatory. Opportunistic cheating occurs when an enticing romantic proposition arises and you take it. Obligatory infidelity occurs when the cheater feels compelled to have sexual intercourse for fear of losing something material or emotional. A married woman who has a "sugar daddy" on the side would be a good example. Virtual infidelity is a recent trend, as people increasingly venture online to look for love or engage in cybersex. While the affairs of virtual cheaters are usually limited to cyberspace, it can still be devastating to a relationship. Then there is emotional infidelity, which does not necessarily involve sexual intercourse. People who are emotionally unfaithful to their partner form a strong romantic friendship with another person in order to fill an emotional need. While emotional infidelity usually involves no physical sex acts, it is still a betrayal. Plus, with escalating levels of intimacy, emotional infidelity often leads to the bedroom.

Men are still slightly more prone to infidelity, but women have been catching up in recent decades. The sexual revolution of the 1960s made it socially acceptable for women to have casual sex; the advent of the birth control pill gave women more control over their reproductive lives; and as more women entered the workforce, they found more romantic opportunities. While men and women are cheating to similar degrees today, they usually cheat for different reasons. Studies suggest that men stray for better sex or more frequent sex, while women stray for emotional reasons. It's often said that men initially start sexual affairs that then turn emotional, while women start emotional affairs that then turn sexual. Of course, this is not an absolute rule. There are plenty of women who begin affairs for the pure physical thrill of it, and there are an equal number of men who have affairs for emotional reassurance or to confirm their own desirability.

Four Phases of an Affair

1. **Contact:** You meet someone who ignites your desire. Flirting suggests a mutual interest.

2. **Debate:** You secretly obsess about your new object of affection. You fantasize about starting a romance, internally debating the risks and rewards.
3. **Dating:** You sneak away with your new love interest for semisecret lunches or drinks after work, often using the "just friends" excuse.
4. **Doing:** A physical affair begins.

Why is monogamy so difficult? With so many people cheating in so many different ways, it seems like the human brain is hardwired for infidelity. This may actually be the case. Anthropological studies suggest that for most of human history, polygamy or polygyny was the norm. The expectation of monogamy only really took root as Judeo-Christianity evolved, and many biologists believe it is a purely social construct. Only a handful of mammal species exhibit a tendency toward monogamy. Most of them are polygamous. In fact, there are few examples of sexual monogamy anywhere in the animal kingdom. About 90 percent of bird species are *socially* monogamous, meaning a male and female will pair-bond, mate, and share territory, but they are not usually *sexually* monogamous. Even the swan, which is revered as a symbol of marriage and fidelity, is not sexually monogamous. DNA studies on swan chicks suggest the "social father" is not the "biological" father in 10–70 percent of the cases.

Our closest animal relatives, the great apes, are polygynous, and human biology suggests we share this sexual heritage. Men have larger bodies and are more aggressive than women, plus, girls reach sexual maturity earlier than boys. These features are typical of mammals living in polygynous systems. The nearly inexhaustible supply of male sperm and limited number of female ovum found in human beings also argues for polygyny and against monogamy. Essentially, men are equipped to spread their genetic seed to almost any willing partner, while women are equipped to be more choosey in mate selection. Some studies have suggested that 10–15 percent of children are conceived during an affair, and recent studies of human paternity tests provide more evidence that there is a lot of hanky-panky going on.

While it is true that some aspects of human biology make monogamy seem "unnatural" and nearly impossible, it is important to remember that nature has also endowed human beings with large and highly developed brains. Unlike the brains of our more promiscuous animal cousins, the human brain has a more elaborate frontal cortex that allows us to reason, exercise good judgment, and override many of our most primitive urges, including sex. The frontal cortex also has multiple connections to the limbic system, the brain's emotional center. These connections allow us to sympathize, show empathy, and

It *Effing Figures

Mommy's Baby, Daddy's Maybe
More than 400,000 paternity tests were conducted in 2006, according to the American Association of Blood Banks. In roughly 28 percent of the tests, the man was excluded from being the biological father.

safeguard each other's feelings. So monogamy may actually be more "natural" than some behaviorists and biologists are willing to admit. It is even possible that our desire for fidelity and the very human tendency toward monogamy has put us on the top rung of the evolutionary ladder.

> If the fish never opened its mouth, it would have never been caught.
> —ANONYMOUS

Spotting a cheater can be extraordinarily difficult. Contrary to what magazines and dating websites report, there are no telltale warning signs. In some cases, a partner may have suspicions, but in most cases the person being cheated on has absolutely no idea. Even when there are suspicions, the situation inherently favors the cheating partner. Questioning from the noncheating partner often prompts a strong denial from the cheater and accusations of mistrust. And after suspicions are raised, cheaters usually learn how to lie more effectively. When questioned, cheaters become more cautious and craft more plausible explanations for their actions or whereabouts, pushing their partners further into the dark.

The emotional toll of infidelity should not be underestimated. It is considered by most to be a severe betrayal of trust that often devastates the self-worth of the noncheating partner. Infidelity often ends in divorces, destroying relationships and entire families.

12 Possible Warning Signs of Infidelity

1. **Beware of friends and coworkers.** Studies show lovers are usually friends or coworkers.
2. **Business travel is high-risk.** Partners are more likely to stray when away from prying eyes.
3. **Your mutual friends start acting odd.** Your friends might know something about your partner that you do not.
4. **Your partner's coworkers are uncomfortable around you.**
5. **Sudden withdrawal.** Your partner is emotionally withdrawn and no longer affectionate or interested in having sex.
6. **Sudden change in appearance.** Cheating partners may have a renewed interest in being more attractive. Sometimes they will lose weight or start an exercise program.
7. **Secretiveness.** Your partner may open a new e-mail account, change passwords, or start erasing text message folders. Remember, people with nothing to hide usually hide nothing.
8. **Finding fault.** To lessen their own guilt, cheaters may point out every flaw in their partners. This helps them rationalize their own bad behavior.
9. **Watch out for guilt gifts and affection.** Sometimes the cheating partner feels so guilty about the affair, they become overly affectionate and generous.
10. **Stories are inconsistent.** Cheaters spin so many lies to cover their liaisons that they inevitably cannot keep their stories straight or provide essential details.
11. **Missing money, strange gifts.** Cheating partners, especially men, often spend a significant amount of money on their lovers. Women often receive extravagant or sentimental gifts from their lovers.

12. **Trust your gut.** Any victim of an affair will tell you, if you
have that sinking feeling, do not dismiss it.

THE *EFFING SOLUTION:
AFFAIR-PROOFING YOUR RELATIONSHIP

It is impossible to completely protect your relationship from
infidelity, but you can take some steps that will minimize the risk
of cheating and reduce damage should an affair occur.

Inform yourself. Examine your partner's past behaviors. Past
behavior is a strong predictor of future behavior, and this rule of
thumb certainly applies to infidelity. People who have cheated in
the past are much more likely to cheat again in the future. As
your relationship becomes more serious, ask your partner about
prior infidelities. Advice columnist Ann Landers put it best, "If
you marry a man who cheats on his wife, you will be married to
a man who cheats on his wife."

Know what is normal. Sex is like a drug. In fact, many addictive
drugs exploit the same exact pleasure pathways inside the brain.
Once you experience an orgasm, you are hardwired to seek
another. Wanting more sex and different sex is completely normal. Surveys suggest that at least 95 percent of men and 80 percent of women in long-term, committed relationships fantasize
about having sex with another person. Fantasy is a very normal
part of the human sexual experience, and it should not be a cause
for alarm in your relationship. If you and your partner do not

take steps to make monogamy exciting, it will inevitably become monotonous. In many cases fantasies serve as healthy and harmless surrogates for infidelity.

Take care of yourself. It is always important to try to look your best for your partner. It boosts your self-esteem and it tells your partner that you are still trying to entice them. If your partner has let his or her appearance deteriorate, have a kind but constructive conversation about making some improvements.

Build true friendships. Seek out other happy couples. Avoid friends who exhibit or encourage bad behavior. Instead, forge friendships with those who are committed to making their relationships work. Focus on building true friendships. Surround yourself with people who are not afraid to tell you when you are acting irresponsibly, being selfish, or just being a fool.

Keep the romance exciting. It is important to keep the romance and passion alive in your relationship. Don't forget about seducing each other. Once you learn what turns your partner on, keep pushing those buttons. You have to deliver the passion you want to receive. Being desired creates desire, and the love will be returned. Be lusty with your partner. Keep dating, keep flirting, and keep the sex exciting.

Find other forms of excitement. Many people who seek affairs are really seeking excitement. They're bored. If you are currently in an "excitement deficit," find other stimulating activities that will add some fun and excitement to your life. Join a gym, a sports team, or even a book club, if that excites you. Take college classes or an art course. Take up skydiving, rock climbing, kayaking, or canoeing. If your partner is also in an excitement deficit, suggest activities you can do as a couple. Just get creative.

Hang out. When all else fails, friendship prevails. Love is grand, but for long-term relationship success, you must genuinely *like* your partner. You must enjoy spending time together while doing everyday things. Having a solid friendship with your spouse is one of the strongest deterrents against infidelity.

Engage your partner. It is natural to want to pull away from your partner if you are thinking of cheating or if you suspect your partner is about to cheat on you. But creating emotional distance at this critical point makes an affair much more likely. Instead, try to engage your partner. Open up the lines of communication and work on cementing your bond.

Make your relationship a top priority. After a while, romantic relationships tend to slip down the priorities list. Move it back up. Talk about your future together. Support each other, be kind, and be thoughtful. Never miss a chance to say "I love you," and celebrate birthdays, holidays, anniversaries, and other relationship milestones.

The #8 *Effing Problem: You've Lost that Loving Feeling

You have fallen out of love—you are sure of it. You might still *love* your partner, but you are no longer "in love" with him or her. Looking back, you recall a time when your partner sent your heart and mind racing with excitement. Every moment seemed magical. But now those times have vanished, and it seems like all the passion was just smoke and mirrors, a cruel trick. You are confused. You feel stuck. You still obsess about your partner but only in a very negative way. You ask yourself over and over, *How could this have happened? How did hot and heavy become cold and lonely? Why am I staying in this relationship? Who am I fooling? Where do I go from here? Am I condemned to a passionless and pointless future?*

The answers to these questions all depend on your definition of love. You cannot fall out of love unless you understand how you fell in love in the first place. To make sense of your love life, you first have to make sense of love.

Why do fools fall in love? That question has inspired musicians, writers, poets, and painters for millennia. While love is the most potent and prized of human emotions, it is also the least understood. Until recently, surprisingly little was known about how and why people love each other. Although most of us are currently in love or have experienced love in the past, very few of us would be able to define exactly what "love" or being "in love" means. And scientists have been equally baffled.

But thanks to recent scientific advances, researchers are now beginning to uncover some of the secrets of the heart. By using new functional MRI brain-scanning techniques, researchers can take live snapshots of the working human brain during various stages of love. For simplicity's sake, let's call these scans brainprints. These new brainprint studies have suggested that love is quite different from our other emotions, like sadness, fear, or anger. In fact, love may not be a true emotion at all. The latest research suggests that love is more likely a strong biological drive, a constant craving, or even an addiction.

Stages of Love

Lust
The first stage of love is driven by the sex hormones testosterone and estrogen. It is a primal and immature stage of love intended for mating. This is also called erotic passion.

Attraction
Also called romantic passion, attraction is really the first stage of "romantic love" and only sometimes follows the lusty stage. Attraction is the whirlwind "falling in love" phase where you idealize your new partner.

Attachment
Attachment is the commitment stage, or lasting stage, of love.

The first stage of love is lust. Lust is a primal urge driven by the sex hormones testosterone and estrogen, and it is not believed to be a true stage of romantic love. It is thought to be a primitive brain reflex designed to peak sexual interest and drive humans—and animals—to reproduce. Sometimes lust leads to romantic love, while at other times it does not. Surprisingly, the brainprint studies indicate that there is very little overlap between lust and romantic love.

Romantic love is the type of love most people are familiar with, and it has two general stages: attraction and attachment.

The attraction stage is the "falling madly in love" phase of romantic relationships. During this time you idealize your new partner and become mildly (or wildly) obsessive. When you see each other, you become giddy with excitement, your face flushes, your heart races, and so do your thoughts. You can't stop thinking about your new partner; you might have trouble concentrating, and you might even act a little crazy. You might also make dumb decisions, overlook faults in your new partner, and take unnecessary risks.

The brainprint studies explain a lot of this behavior. During the attraction stage, the pleasure and reward centers of your brain are being bathed in the feel-good neurotransmitter dopamine. In fact, the brainprint of attraction looks very similar to the pattern seen when people eat chocolate, win a lot of money, have orgasms, or do drugs like cocaine and heroin. Norepinephrine and adrenaline are also released during the attraction stage, and are believed to help you stay focused on your new partner, heighten your awareness, and boost sexual excitement. The pleasure generated during the attachment phase is extraordinarily powerful, and like an addictive rush, it leaves you wanting more. Based on the brainprint analysis, falling in love seems a bit self-serving; you don't fall in love because your new partner is wonderful, but because your new partner makes you feel wonderful.

With time the brain becomes accustomed to the effects of attraction as the dopamine-driven love charge loses some of its voltage. Your brain chemistry begins to transition from attraction

True *Effing Fact

Madly in Love

Love is mostly a right-sided brain phenomenon. The right hemisphere is the less rational but more creative half of the brain. This may be the reason why people tend to act so irrationally when they are falling in love, and why love inspires so many songs, paintings, and poems.

to the attachment phase. The attachment phase of romantic love is characterized by increasing levels of commitment and intimacy. Partners in attachment connect with each other on a new emotional level, and a true friendship often develops. During attachment parts of the brain are bathed in oxytocin, a neurotransmitter and hormone known as the cuddle chemical. Another hormone, called vasopressin, reinforces that bond while the body's natural painkillers, called endorphins, increase feelings of security and comfort. This chemical cascade creates a long-term love imprint, but with dropping dopamine levels, some passion is lost for the sake of permanence.

As love evolves over time, the brain chemistry pattern changes from lust and attraction to attachment—and it stays there. Even most long-term couples who claim they are still madly, wildly in love are in attachment. In fact, the chemical brainprints seen in couples who have been in long-term love relationships usually don't resemble the attraction pattern at all. They more closely resemble the brainprints of close family relationships.

Although we still know very little about love, it is important to understand what we do know. Every couple moves from attraction to attachment at different speeds, and nobody should expect to have that high-octane, mind-blowing passion once an intimate attachment has developed. Confusing and even disturbing questions about the depth of your love are completely normal in any long-term relationship, and knowing some of the science may help you keep your feelings in perspective.

Signs You May Be Falling Out of Love

1. You are physically repulsed by your partner.
2. You cringe before kissing.
3. You constantly point out your partner's faults.
4. You feel like a fraud.
5. You married for money, sex, or security.
6. Your basic emotional needs are not being met.
7. You don't respect your partner.
8. You no longer care if your partner has sex with someone else.
9. You avoid talking about the future.
10. You are never happy at home.

THE *EFFING SOLUTION: HOW TO MAKE A LOVE U-TURN

Unfortunately, it is easy to fall in love but hard to stay in love. As your relationship changes with time, you must change along with it—and change requires work. If you have not been adjusting and growing within the relationship, now is the time to start. Falling out of love is usually a painfully slow process, so time is on your side. You can make a love U-turn as long as you keep your expectations realistic. You will probably never be able to recapture the passion and excitement of your early courtship, but you can still rebuild a love affair that is full of passion and intimacy.

Create a love concept. You must define exactly what you mean by love. Love is an abstract concept for most people, and writing some thoughts on paper will help you see what you have in your relationship and what you are lacking. Write down an explicit definition of love—the actions that you consider demonstrate love—and all of your other love expectations.

Take a reality check. Compare your love concept to what you read in books, watch on television, and see in the movies. If your love concept is strikingly similar to the dramatic love concept, you have been terribly misled. If books and the mainstream media accurately portrayed the amount of tedium in real-life romances, you wouldn't want to read or watch. Make sure you are not holding your relationship up to a ridiculous Hollywood standard.

Identify changes. Thinking back to a happier time in the relationship, write down all the ways both you and your partner have changed. Were you more attentive, seductive, and forgiving? Include all of the positive and negative changes. Identify ways in which the relationship has fundamentally changed. Are other obligations interfering with your ability to love each other? Have children entered the picture? Has one partner lost a job or received a promotion? Examine how all these changes are related and try to figure out a few easy solutions.

Time to talk. It might seem premature, but once you have developed a realistic love concept and identified ways your relationship has changed, it is time to have a thoughtful and candid conversation with your partner. Tell your partner that you are having serious doubts about your commitment to each other based on the changes you are seeing in the relationship. Keep your conversation solution oriented, and assure your partner that you are committed to improving your love bond. You might feel like you have not gathered enough information for this conversation, but your partner may have similar concerns. When two people drift away from each other, they drift away at twice the speed. Remember, romance is a partnership, and the earlier you involve your partner, the better.

Active loving. Love is a feeling, but it is also an action. It is a noun and a verb—and verbs usually imply action. Don't be passive about love. It will not magically appear in your relationship. You must give love to get it. Make specific and unambiguous efforts to demonstrate your love for your partner at least once a day. Like a bank account, you have to deposit some love before you can withdraw it. You must start giving the love you want in return.

Starve your resentment. Your perceptions become your reality. Don't focus on feelings of resentment and hostility. When people fall in love, they often develop a positive obsession for their partners, and it is constant excitement. While falling out of love, the obsession turns negative and becomes constant resentment. Stop obsessing. You have to be active about blocking these negative thoughts, otherwise they just grow with time and the obsession intensifies. Block the negative thoughts, replace them, or otherwise distract yourself. Keep yourself busy with positive activities, or perhaps try meditation.

Stay positive. Instead of complaining about all the faults in your partner and problems in your relationship, do your best to acknowledge the positive. Talk about what is right with your partner and your relationship. When speaking with family or friends, avoid the temptation of turning it into a gripe session. Mention all the positive things your partner is doing for you. Your friends and family might just comment on how lucky you are. Getting positive feedback from close friends and family will help you better appreciate the value of your partner.

Let it go. Don't hold on to past resentments. If something happened in the past and you are still committed to making your relationship work, you must let the resentment go. Base all of your judgments about the relationship on the present actions of your partner.

Seduce each other. To add some passion into your lives, make sure you are seducing each other on a regular basis. Look your best. Express desire. If your sex life has turned boring, be open to spicing it up a bit. Have fun, make love, and hang out like you used to.

What is missing in passion, make up for with intimacy. While you may never recapture the passion you had with your partner in the first years of dating, you should make efforts to become increasingly intimate. Like passionate love, being understood and cherished is also a fundamental human desire. Feed your partner's desire for intimacy—it is the glue of all long-term love relationships. Concentrate on safeguarding your partner and attending to their emotional needs.

THE #9 *EFFING PROBLEM: YOU HAVE A DATING DISORDER

The dance floor is getting crowded. According to the U.S. Census Bureau, there are more than 100 million unmarried Americans. There are approximately 20 million divorced singles, 15 million singles over the age of sixty-five, 10 million single mothers, and 2.2 million single fathers. Some of them try speed dating, blind dating, social mixers, and singles cruises. Forty million of them are using online dating services and social networking websites to make new romantic connections. Many others allow friends and relatives to play matchmaker, and every night of the week bars, restaurants, and nightclubs across the country are packed with singles looking for dates. The single life has become so celebrated there is even a National Unmarried and Single Americans Week that is held yearly in September.

True *Effing Fact

Love alone is not enough to keep a relationship strong, according to an Australian National University survey of more than 2,500 couples.

The dating scene has also become more complicated and confusing. The rules of the game have undergone a radical transformation in the last few decades. While men have always dated younger women, the age gap is widening. And as the recent "cougar" trend demonstrates, it has become more acceptable for women to seek younger romantic partners. Compared to previous generations of single women, today's single women are more confident in expressing their sexuality and more open to engaging in sexual relationships without serious commitment. Dating multiple partners at the same time was frowned upon by generations past, but it is quickly becoming the norm, especially among online daters. Many teens and twenty-somethings are not even dating in the traditional sense, dismissing it as an antiquated ritual. Instead, they are opting for noncommittal "hookups."

With so many dating outlets, options, and competition, finding your perfect match seems near impossible—like trying to snare the perfect fish out of the sea while using lousy bait and one tiny hook. But if you have been fishing and have been unable to reel in a partner, you might be making some critical dating errors.

10 Common Dating Mistakes that Both Men and Women Make

1. Showing up late
2. Talking too much about yourself
3. Talking about your ex
4. Not listening

5. Sloppy appearance
6. Drinking too much
7. Taking the relationship too fast
8. Being rude, arrogant, or aloof
9. Being too picky
10. Pushing for sex or having sex too quickly

Tool trouble. Men will often try too hard to impress a woman with their intellect, machismo, or money. They may show off their knowledge on a particular subject, overinflate their pectoral muscles, or overspend on extravagant dinners or gifts, hoping it will literally charm a woman's clothes off. Men are more likely to drink heavily on a date, and women often complain they don't listen. If a man overexpresses confidence, women often interpret it as arrogance or insecurity. Some men really are arrogant and insecure. Numerous sex surveys indicate that men are much more interested in having casual sex or a one-night stand. Women also complain that men lack manners, touch them inappropriately, and push for sex way too hard and way too early. Other men are too wishy-washy, too desperate, and not assertive enough.

Miss-Takes. On dates talkative women may have a tendency to dominate the conversation, bringing up past relationships or unpacking other emotional baggage. Men often complain that women reveal too much about themselves too soon. When the conversation shifts to the man, it becomes an interrogation, as if the date were a job interview. Men commonly report that women put too much emphasis on material items, like the kind of car a man drives, the watch he is wearing, or how much money he earns. And while men push women for sex, women push for commitment, and many men feel pressured. When the date is over, many women forget to say "thank you," and that often makes men feel unappreciated or used.

Despite the drawbacks, dating can be very exciting. While modern culture has changed, human behavior has not changed. We all hope to connect with someone special. Being in love is vitally important to most people, and the promise of real partnership is as alluring today as it has ever been.

THE *EFFING SOLUTION: HOW TO BE A MATE MAGNET

Date yourself first. Your relationship with another person actually begins long before you even lay eyes on each other. It starts while you are single. Spend some time alone. Try to find out more about yourself—try to pin down your likes and dislikes, your fears and hopes. Address any personal problems that may be interfering with romantic relationships and try to correct them. Remember: relationships are not a guarantee of happiness—in fact, many of them end unhappily. So approach singlehood enthusiastically. By getting to know yourself on a more personal level, addressing emotional or psychological issues, and developing interests and hobbies, you will be much more appealing to the opposite sex.

Be charming, not alarming. Surveys reveal that most women have shot a flirty glance at a man they were attracted to, but he never approached her. Though women have gotten more comfortable about asking men out on a date, it is still usually up to the man to make the first move. Men need to learn how to recognize the flirty glance and have the confidence to act on it. Men should resist the urge to use primitive "pickup" lines when approaching an attractive woman. Almost invariably the pickup line backfires. Pickup lines with sexual innuendo, whistling, and catcalling always come off as creepy. Surveys suggest that the only pickup lines that work on women are the ones that make them laugh—and even those don't work often.

True *Effing Pickup Lines

Pickup lines usually guarantee a romantic rejection. When they work, they usually involve absurdly dumb humor. Use these at your own risk!

"Are you from Tennessee? Cause you're the only ten I see."

"Can I buy you a drink, or do you just want the money?"

"I suffer from amnesia. Do I come here often?"

"Do you believe in love at first sight, or do I have to walk by you again?"

"Hi, who's your friend?"

"Can I see your shirt's tag? Hmm, just what I thought—made in heaven."

Give men what they *really* want. When it comes to choosing a mate, physical attractiveness is extremely important for both men and women. But studies on speed daters have shown that men have a "shoot for the moon" strategy, tending to select the most attractive women for follow-up dates. Average-looking and unattractive women are brushed aside, even if they meet all of the men's pre-stated personality preferences. Simply put, women with "great personalities" don't get very many dates. But they don't have to be skinny supermodels either! Men are not very selective. In fact, men are less selective than women, favoring all women who meet a certain attractiveness "threshold." With makeup, hairstyle, and a wide range of fashions, women can dramatically alter their appearance and maximize their physical attractiveness. What about a woman's weight? Body silhouette studies suggest overall that men do find overweight or obese women less attractive than thinner women; however, female bodies with average dimensions are chosen as the most desirable. Age is an important consideration. Men consistently find younger, fertile women more sexually attractive than older women. This is thought to be an evolutionary reproductive strategy aimed at increasing the likelihood of a successful pregnancy. A woman's earning potential does not appear to be a strong dating consideration for most men. Loyalty was the personality trait ranked most highly prized by men in the Great Male Survey (2009) from AskMen.com.

True *Effing Fact

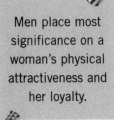

Men place most significance on a woman's physical attractiveness and her loyalty.

Give women what they _really_ want. Women, as you might suspect, are a bit more complicated in their mate selection. Contrary to popular belief, women are _more_ selective than men when it comes to physical appearance. Dating studies have found that women generally choose romantic partners who are equally attractive or more attractive than themselves. But that's only a small part of what entices women. A study from the University of Texas at Austin found that women base mate selection primarily on a combination of four factors: good genes, earning potential, parenting skills, and loyalty. Their research suggests that women seek to maximize the combination of these four criteria when looking for a man. Good health genes are reflected in a man's overall attractiveness, and several studies have shown women are physically attracted to men whose immunity genes are different from their own. This preference for complementary immune DNA is thought to be an instinctual reproductive strategy. It is mediated through pheromones, and it increases the odds of having healthier babies with broader immune systems.

It should come as no surprise that money matters to women. It's often said that women are sex objects and men are _success_ objects, and the available science suggests that might be true— at least to some extent. A man's income is an important consideration for many women, especially for very attractive women. Extremely attractive women are drawn to the wealthiest men. A 2006 University of Chicago study of online daters found that men with incomes exceeding $250,000 a year generated significantly more interest than those making under $50,000. A more recent study conducted by British researchers at Newcastle University also found that women have significantly more orgasms with wealthy men, and rich men were better lovers. This fondness for wealthier men is probably instinctual and certainly does not suggest that all women are calculating gold diggers. The female preference for "good providers" is seen throughout the animal kingdom. From chimps to chipmunks, males that provide the most tend to mate the most. But this can work to a man's advantage. Men do not have many options to improve their physical appearance, but they can always increase their bank account and assets. A man's personality is important for women. While surveys have suggested that women value a sense of humor in a man, they seek out loyal men and those with strong parenting skills.

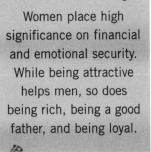

True *Effing Fact

Women place high significance on financial and emotional security. While being attractive helps men, so does being rich, being a good father, and being loyal.

More hooks, more fish. There are more dating outlets than ever before, and you should explore as many as you can. Do not limit yourself to the traditional bars, nightclubs, and introductions from friends. Get over your fear of online dating or go mingle with strangers at mixers and other social events. Take a few classes at the local college or chat with people on the street or in the supermarket.

Live in expectation. Always be optimistic. Someone special is out there looking for you. Keep your eyes and your options open. Enjoy the experience of meeting new people without putting too much emphasis on forming a romantic relationship. In most cases relationships don't suddenly appear, they evolve. Embrace the "friends first" philosophy and let the connecting begin.

Have a sense of humor. Being happy and having a good sense of humor is essential for all new relationships. Many women say they can't resist a man who can make them laugh, and having a good sense of humor consistently ranks high on the list of desirable personality traits women seek in men. Men also appreciate a sense of humor in women, just not as much.

First impressions matter. Both men and women make a judgment about a potential mate within three seconds of meeting. Always try your best to look your best.

Harness the "power of new." Self-improvement coaches often tell people to harness the power of now. When it comes to dating, it is equally important to harness the power of new. Go to new restaurants or clubs, get a new job, a new set of friends, or better yet, move to a new town or city.

Top Five Cities for Singles

Each year Forbes.com ranks the top forty cities in the United States for singles based on the city's number of single people, nightlife, job growth, coolness, and other factors. Below are the rankings from 2009.

1. New York City
2. Boston
3. Chicago

4. Seattle
5. Washington, D.C.

THE #10 *EFFING PROBLEM: YOUR MATE IS A MANIAC

Let's face it. Sometimes people make horrible decisions when choosing a romantic partner. The BTK killer, Dennis Rader, was married for thirty-three years. Ted Bundy was engaged to be married before he went on his murderous rampage. Scott Peterson, who was convicted in 2005 of killing his pregnant wife, Laci Peterson, is reportedly flooded with marriage proposals even as he sits on death row. More than 1.3 million women and more than 800,000 men are assaulted by a spouse or domestic partner each year in the United States. If you are in an abusive situation, you must get help and get out.

THE *EFFING SOLUTION: GET HELP AND GET OUT

The abuse is not your fault. Stop blaming yourself. If you are in an abusive relationship, you must act now and you must leave now. If you have children, do not leave them at home with the abuser. Notify your local authorities and let loved ones know what you are going through. Immediately call the National Domestic Violence Hotline (NDVH) and ask for specific advice.

The hotline is free, and help is available twenty-four hours a day, seven days a week—even on holidays. The NDVH website offers essential information on how to create a "safety plan" while living with an abuser, how to leave safely, and how to cope with the aftermath of leaving an abusive relationship. They can be contacted at the National Domestic Violence Hotline, 1-800-799-SAFE (7233) or 1-800-787-3224 (TTY), or visit www.ndvh.org.

3 No *Effing Money

Research suggests that money does buy a certain degree of happiness. Economic studies show that having financial security increases overall life satisfaction. As nations become wealthier, the individual citizens become happier. Gallup polls from around the world suggest that life satisfaction is highest in the richest countries and lowest in the poorest countries, making Zimbabwe and Burundi two of the unhappiest places on Earth. In the United States, people who have an income of $75,000 or more are twice as likely to report being "very happy" compared to those with an income of $25,000 or less. And people who make the most money are the happiest, with 90 percent declaring themselves as "very happy."

True*Effing Fact

Money Matters
Wealthy men give women more orgasms, according to a 2009 report from Australian researchers, and surveys also suggest rich men and wealthy women have more satisfying sex lives.

But you don't have to be a multimillionaire to be happy. Wealth does not appear to increase happiness in a linear fashion. While people who make more than $20 million each year are significantly happier than those who make $20,000, they are not significantly happier than those who make $250,000. So being a multimillionaire will not make you much happier than being financially comfortable. And that million-dollar smile may not last forever either. Studies on lottery winners find that happiness returns to baseline within five years of hitting the financial jackpot. Some experts have suggested that money only buys lasting happiness when a valuable experience is gained.

Money is clearly not essential for many important things—loving your children, for instance. But most of us enjoy having more money than we need, and being broke is a real bummer. Here's how to start taking better care of your finances.

True *Effing Fact

A study published in the *British Medical Journal* in 1999 found that billionaires live 3.5 years longer than the average American man.

THE #1 *EFFING PROBLEM: FUDGETING

"I don't know where my money goes."

How often have you said this? Household finances remain the single most common source of frustration in American homes. We are a nation of overspending undersavers who do not know how to budget ourselves. Every Fortune 500 company operates on a budget, and so do most other successful businesses. Our local, state, and federal governments all operate on budgets. Foreign governments—even the crooked ones—budget their money, too. So do public school systems, colleges, and universities. The evidence is overwhelming: budgets are essential to securing finances and building wealth. But very few people budget their household finances. And those who do establish a budget often have a hard time sticking to it. Most Americans know how much money they make each year, but have little idea about how much money they spend. Do you know how much you spent on ATM fees this week, this month, or last year? If you had a budget, you would. This dangerous disconnection between your incoming and outgoing finances is called "fudgeting."

Signs of Fudgeting

1. You're living from paycheck to paycheck.
2. Money seems to leak from your wallet, your purse, or your bank accounts.
3. You pay bills with credit cards.
4. You have a "buy now, pay later" mentality.
5. You keep anticipating a financial windfall.
6. You have no clear financial goals.
7. You hide your spending from your spouse (financial infidelity).
8. As your income has increased, so have your expenses.
9. If you have fallen behind on paying utilities, rent, or mortgage bills, you are deep in the fudge zone.

Most people avoid budgeting because it forces them to confront foolish spending habits. Ignorance is bliss, especially when it comes to money. Like the word "diet," the word "budget" can be discouraging to some people, and many personal finance experts recommend calling your budget a "spending plan" instead. That may be a good idea, because establishing a budget is not really about restricting finances, but about allocating them. A budget is a blueprint for where and how you want to spend your money, and it is one of the surest ways to financial freedom. Budgets allow you to enjoy the money you have, without any guilt.

THE *EFFING SOLUTION: BASIC BUDGETING

If you want to control your financial future, establishing a household budget is essential. Studies have shown that the average American household spends 10 percent more money than they earn each year, meaning that most Americans are living in a budget deficit, and very few are living in a budget surplus. If you do not stick to a budget, you will always be spending too much.

Creating a budget does not have to be daunting. For most people a pencil, notebook, and calculator will suffice. Software programs like Quicken and Microsoft Money can make budget making easy, and are especially helpful for complex budgets. There are also plenty of websites that offer free advice on how to create a basic household budget, and many of them offer free budget templates and worksheets. But you can establish an effective basic budget with little or no help at all. These ten easy steps will help you create a very effective budget and put you on the road to financial security.

Step 1

Start now! Whether it is at the beginning, middle, or end of the month—even if it is the end of the year—get started on your budget. Today is always the best time to start tracking your spending habits and improving your financial health. Don't worry! Things are rarely as bad as they seem. Just make a decision to budget yourself, start keeping track of your expenses, and collect all your bills and financial data.

Step 2

Income analysis. Total all of your major sources of income. Keep it simple. Don't spend hours trying to predict growth in your IRA, your stock portfolio, or home equity. Just add your paycheck to other significant sources of monthly income. If you have a rental property, count the rent as income.

Step 3

Track your expenses. Identify all your expenses by keeping a log. Keeping a record of what you are spending your money on will automatically make you spend less. So write down everything that you spend your money on for each month, including lunches, coffee, groceries, and bills. Once you have identified all of your bills and small and large purchases for the month, add all of your expenses.

Step 4

Do the math. Subtract your total monthly expenses from your total monthly income. DON'T CRY or GIVE UP if your expenses exceed your income. You have a lot of company. The purpose of a budget is to help you and millions of other Americans get out of the red and into the black.

> **Total Income -**
> **Total Expenses =**
> **Household Savings**

Step 5

Expense analysis. Now divide your total expenses into fixed expenses and variable expenses. Fixed expenses are often compulsory and usually don't change much from month to month. Variable expenses are less compulsory and change significantly from month to month.

Fixed Expenses

Debt: Student loans, mortgage, rent, car
Leases: Car, boat, home
Insurance: Home, car, health
Service Contracts: Cell phone, alarm systems, lawn care, Internet, cable, gym, child care
Municipal Fees: Sewer, garbage

Variable Expenses

Groceries, restaurants, alcohol
Painting, yard care, home improvement
Electricity, gas, water
Clothing, laundry services
Toys, sporting equipment
Car maintenance, home repair

Step 6

Lower your variable expenses. For a few months concentrate on lowering your variable expenses. This can save you hundreds of dollars each month and thousands each year. Turn off the lights to lower your electricity bill. Set your home thermostat at 78 degrees in the summer and 60 degrees during the winter. Adjust the thermostat to comfort when you are home. Cook most meals at home and bring a brown-bag lunch to work. Buy sale items at the supermarket and use coupons. Avoid convenience or impulse shopping. Do basic home repairs, lawn care, and painting yourself.

Step 7

Apply savings to bad debt. If you have any credit card debt or other high interest rate payments, apply the savings from your reduced variable expenses to the balance. You must get out of credit card debt. Call your credit card company and ask for a lower interest rate. If you don't have any credit card debt, great! Start saving your money in a high-interest savings account.

Step 8

Reduce fixed expenses. Most fixed costs are not completely fixed. Closely examine your fixed expenses and explore ways to reduce them. If you are married with two incomes and paying for child care, you may want to investigate the possibility of one parent working from home or not working at all. Perhaps a relative could help with child care. Home mortgages can be refinanced and loan interest rates can be renegotiated. Renters may seek a roommate. Streamline and downsize your service plans for cable, Internet, and cell phone.

Step 9

Involve others. If you are setting the budget for a family, it is important to make everyone a part of the process. Make sure everyone agrees on the terms of the budget and all needs are being met. Family members can be a great source of support; plus, having a written budget helps prevent conflicts over household spending.

Step 10

Set financial goals. Living within a tight budget can be unpleasant, and that's why it is important to incentivize the process. Set financial goals for yourself or for your family. Each month add your newfound budget surplus to the financial goal. You could save for retirement, a vacation, a new car, a new home, or college tuition—just make sure you save your surplus and apply it toward something worthwhile.

THE #2 *EFFING PROBLEM: NO SAVINGS

In 1959 Americans saved roughly 11 percent of their disposable income, according to commerce department statistics. From 1980 through 1994 the U.S. savings rate averaged around 8 percent, but then it started to decline. In 2001, the savings rate dropped more steeply as more Americans tapped into their savings to buy cars, investment homes, and other big ticket items. By 2005 the savings rate had plummeted to *negative* 0.5 percent! People were spending more than they earned. The savings rate dipped even further in 2006 to *negative* 1 percent. These were the first negative U.S. savings rates seen since the Great Depression. But after the simultaneous collapse of the housing and stock markets in 2008, average Americans started saving again. The savings rate rebounded to a little more than 5 percent during 2009. That sounds pretty good. But compare that with the 10 percent seen throughout Europe, and the 25–30 percent national savings rate seen in China.

The average American family has just a few thousand dollars in the bank and little saved for retirement. According to the 2009 Retirement Confidence Survey, conducted by the Employee Benefit Research Institute (EBRI), 40 percent of all workers have less than ten thousand dollars in retirement savings. Most Americans will long outlive their savings, making them dependent on government assistance or family members to cover most of their expenses in older age. While your family might come to your rescue, don't count on the federal government. Currently Social Security covers about one-third of the expenses for the average U.S. retiree, and predictions suggest that the funds will be exhausted by 2041.

So why aren't you saving your money?

Clearly, keeping up with the Joneses is keeping some people in debt. Car ownership is at an all-time high—1.9 cars per household—and homes have gotten larger and more elaborate. The average American home now has more television sets than people! But this obvious hyperconsumerism is probably not the only reason for your personal savings failure. Several other factors are involved. Television creates desire by bombarding you with images of near impossible affluence and advertisements for products you don't really need. Costs for housing, healthcare, and education have also skyrocketed over the last few decades, and more Americans are facing immediate financial challenges. You might not be making enough money to save a significant portion of your income. These day-to-day expenses have made it much more difficult to contribute to long-term savings, and the gap between the rich and the poor has never been wider. You have also become increasingly detached from many of your financial transactions. Electronic transfers and debit and credit cards allow you to pay bills and buy things without ever physically handling any money. Rest assured, if you had to go to the bank or shell out cash for every purchase, you would think twice before buying something stupid. Of course, you might also be one of those remorseless spenders who believe money should be freely spent and enjoyed. This financial strategy works perfectly well until you are too old to work and flat broke.

True *Effing Fact

Median income for the average CEO of an S&P 500 company was $10.4 million in 2008 or $28,493 each day of the year. Median income for the average U.S. worker in 2008 was just $32,390, or roughly $89 each day.

The *Effing Solution: How to Save Yourself

If possible, open a high-yield savings account. High-yield savings accounts offer higher interest rates than basic savings accounts, although they usually come with more restrictions and higher minimum balance requirements. But they can really pay off. According to the Consumer Federation of America, consumers lose $30–50 billion each year by not switching their funds to a high-interest savings account. Online banks usually offer the highest interest rates because they have lower overhead and fewer administrative costs. Money market accounts are high-interest savings accounts, but they allow a limited number of checks to be written each month. Of course, some may choose to maximize their contributions to their employee-sponsored 401(k) plan, or open an IRA account. All of these are fine options. Just start saving.

How much should you be saving? Most experts recommend 10 percent of each paycheck. If you cannot do 10 percent, do 5 percent, then increase it when you can. Make sure you get rid of bad debt first! Apply at least 10 percent of your paycheck to bad debt and live off of the remaining 90 percent. This is what financial experts call the "pay yourself first" method, and it works.

It is also important to make deposits into your savings account convenient while making withdrawals inconvenient. Don't ask for an ATM card for your savings account. Don't have overdraft protection. In fact, don't link your savings to your checking account at all. Do ask your bank to directly deposit a portion of your paycheck into your savings account each pay period.

The sooner you start saving, the sooner your financial future will improve. The good news is you can dramatically lower your month-to-month expenses by using a little creative cost-cutting and making a few sacrifices. By making changes to the three biggest monthly costs, you can really maximize your savings. For most people these are housing, transportation, and food.

Here's Where Your Money Goes

The following annual expenses are based on the average American household in 2007 with a pretax income of $63,091:

Housing	$16,920
Transportation	$8,758
Food at Home	$3,465
Health care	$2,853
Dining out	$2,668
Entertainment	$2,698
Clothing	$1,881

That's $39,243. More than half of total income *before* taxes, and not including education, utilities, and incidentals.

(*Source:* 2009 Bureau of Labor Statistics' Consumer Expenditure Survey)

How to save on housing. If you can accommodate a roommate, get one. A good roommate can chop most major monthly expenses in half. If you rent, think about moving to a lower-rent apartment. If you own a home, refinance your mortgage and get a lower interest rate. This can save you a significant sum of money month after month. Think about downsizing or relocating to an area with lower property taxes. If your home has declined in value, a reassessment may lower your property taxes. Compare rates of homeowner insurance policies.

How to save on transportation: Buy a used car and run it into the ground. Biking or walking to work is a wonderful option if you live close enough to your job. If you live too far, consider moving closer to work. Trade in your gas guzzler for a more economical car and buy the cheapest gas in your immediate neighborhood. Maintain your vehicles properly to prevent costly repairs. Streamline your auto insurance or find cheaper coverage. If you travel on toll roads, see if there are alternate routes. Explore ways of working from home. If you are in a two-car household, consider the option of downsizing to just one car. That might seem drastic, but joining a carpool or using mass transit can make it easy. Mass transit is an excellent option. It's good for your wallet, good for the environment, and good for the local economy.

True *Effing Fact

Mass transit helps save money and the environment. But it might also save your life. Mass transit is the safest way to travel, according to the American Public Transportation Association, and the National Safety Council estimates that riding a bus is 170 times safer than driving a car.

How to save on food. Do most of your cooking at home. Scan your refrigerator and pantry before heading to the supermarket. Don't go to the supermarket hungry. Shop for groceries once a week, go shopping alone, and bring a shopping list. This strategy is the best way to prevent impulse purchases. Buy in bulk. Don't buy sale items just because they are on sale. Clip coupons and use them in combination with supermarket sales. Print coupons off the Internet. Combine manufacturer coupons with store coupons. Try generic or store-brand items. Don't waste leftovers. Brown-bag your lunch. Don't buy bottled water—drink from the tap.

When dining out, take advantage of restaurant specials. If you have young children, dine out on nights when kids eat free. Share meals and use coupons. Websites like Restaurants.com offer discounted gift certificates, which can save you up to 80 percent. Avoid ordering à la carte. Don't treat others. If you eat out often, think about joining a restaurant club. Lunch often costs much less than dinner for the same meal at the same restaurant—so plan social lunches instead of dinners. Avoid alcohol at restaurants; one glass of wine can cost as much as an entrée. Instead, save the nightcap and dessert for home. Check your bill for accuracy, and don't forget the leftovers!

Wherever and whatever you decide to eat, eat less. Americans are eating way too much food. Cutting back on the amount of food you eat will be good for your waistline and your bottom line.

How to save money on entertainment. Think about reducing or eliminating your cable bill. Many television shows are now available on the Internet for free. Bundling your Internet, phone, and cable television can save some money too. Prepaid cell phones are helpful if you frequently go over minutes. Get rid of your land telephone line. Use Skype.com or another service for international calls. Get a calling card. Rent movies at home. If you enjoy going to the movie theater, go to matinees and bring your own candy. Search the local newspaper and websites for free events. Visit museums and attend free concerts. Have a day at the park with your family or friends. Go hiking, fishing, camping, or rafting. If you read a lot of books, buy used books at Amazon.com or dust off your old library card. Volunteer to help at charitable organizations. If you are a sports fan, buy discount or group tickets and avoid buying season tickets. If you're a fitness freak, check out the local community center; memberships are often cheaper than commercial health clubs. Colleges and universities also offer many low-cost educational and cultural events. To get away from the kids for date night with your spouse, try team babysitting. Just ask another couple with children to watch your kids and then return the favor. Cancel gym memberships you do not use.

How to save money on clothing. Avoid using store credit. Shop with cash or with your debit card, and only buy clothes you can afford. Check newspapers for specials and look for online bargains. Buy your seasonal clothes off-season. Sign up for the e-mail newsletters of your favorite retailers—many offer discounts to subscribers. Discount retailers like Target, Walmart, Kmart, and TJ Maxx offer stylish in-house brands and even designer clothing at a fraction of the cost. Outlets, thrift stores, and garage sales are also a good source of clothing bargains. Be open to hand-me-downs, and sell items you no longer wear. Take proper care of the clothing you wear.

How to save money on utilities. Unplug most of your appliances while not in use. Some experts estimate that as much as 40 percent of electricity is consumed when electronic devices are plugged in but turned off. Compact fluorescent lightbulbs (CFLs) are a bit pricey, but over the lifetime of the bulb, they save about sixty dollars. Keep your thermostat set to 78 degrees during the summer and adjust to comfort when home. During the winter keep your thermostat set to 60 degrees. For every one degree, you can lower your heating bill by 5 percent. Service your furnace as scheduled and change the filter on your air conditioner each summer. Block off any drafts in the house. Keep the lights off in rooms that are not being used and use automatic timers. Use cold water for most of your laundry. Low flow faucets, showerheads, and toilets can help you save on your water bill.

How to save money on other stuff. Collect your change and deposit it into your savings account every few months. Consolidating student loans can save a few percentage points of interest and possibly thousands of dollars over the life of the loan. If you are getting an income tax refund each year, that means you are paying too much to Uncle Sam and are losing money—sometimes a lot of money. Adjust your withholdings.

Seven Deadly Sins of Savings

1. Financing your dreams with credit cards or high-interest loans
2. Spending creep: as income increases, so does your spending
3. Overpaying for anything
4. Financial infidelity
5. Envy: trying to keep up with the Joneses
6. Emotional or impulse shopping
7. Paying for things you do not use

THE #3 *EFFING PROBLEM: NO EMERGENCY FUND

Root canals happen. So do bad backs, broken bones, and car crashes. What would happen if you suddenly got sick or lost your job? What if you were hit with a massive tax bill, a lawsuit, or a nasty divorce? Where would the money come from to repair a broken-down car or home appliance? How about valuables lost to theft or fire? Life is full of surprises and emergencies—it is not a matter of *if* these kinds of misfortunes will hit you, but *when*. The financial burden of these emergencies is often compounded by lost wages due to missed work. Are you prepared for one of these incidents right now? Probably not. Most Americans are just one serious illness, accident, job loss, or lawsuit away from the poorhouse. That's why it is critical to start an emergency fund and make it grow.

It ***Effing** Figures

Harvard University researchers say health problems and medical bills were the root cause of 62 percent of all personal bankruptcies filed in 2007.

A national survey conducted by Bankrate.com found more than 60 percent of Americans do not have any funds set aside for emergencies. Men in general have a bit more survival money saved up than women do, according to the survey, and older folks are better prepared than younger folks. Not surprising, people who make the least amount of money are the least likely to have an emergency account. Unfortunately, they need emergency funds the most. Low-income earners are more likely to lose their jobs, drive older automobiles, suffer an accident, and get sick.

The benefit of having an emergency fund is threefold: it provides an immediate source of cash for several months in the event of an emergency; it prevents you from using credit cards or high-interest loans to get out of your predicament; and it stops you from tapping into your 401(k) or IRA. Having an emergency fund can also give you a psychological boost by providing a great deal of financial security. Stop making excuses. This is really important. If you don't have $100 to start an emergency account, where do you think you will get the $1,400 for a radiator repair?

THE *EFFING SOLUTION: EMERGENCY FUND 911

There is no reason to panic, but plan for the worst-case scenario and get started on your emergency fund right away. Make sure that the fund also earns as much money as it can. Open up a separate high-interest savings account or money market account and start socking money away. Start small and make regular deposits until you reach your funding goal. Just like your savings account, it takes time, effort, and sacrifice to build a healthy emergency fund. Ideally, your emergency fund should contain enough money to cover all of your living expenses for six months. Most financial experts believe that having less than three months' savings is grossly inadequate.

Emergency Fund

Financial experts recommend having at least three months of expenses in your emergency fund—preferably six.

That amount of money may seem daunting, but don't let that stop you. Having *something* in the bank to cover emergencies is still much better than having *nothing*. Just get started, be patient, and be consistent. Of course, be careful. Many accidents and illnesses can be prevented. Some find it helpful to use good fortune to build their account. If you come into money, receive a bonus at work, or even get a birthday check, deposit it directly into your emergency fund. The same goes for wedding checks and that tax refund (which you should not be getting, by the way). Just keep at it. Unlike your savings account, your emergency fund should be easily accessible. It's also important to replenish

Good *Effing Advice

> Expect the unexpected:
> start an emergency fund.

your emergency fund as you use it, and adjust your balance accordingly as your monthly expenses increase or decrease.

An important note about debt: If you are in a substantial amount of debt, it is best to pay off your debts before building a savings account or an emergency account. If you do not, the high-interest rate you will be paying on your debt will outpace the gains from a high-interest savings or money market account. Paying down your high-interest debts first is almost always the best financial maneuver. Once those debts are gone, you will have more money to put in your savings and emergency accounts.

THE #4 *EFFING PROBLEM: BRAINLESS BUYING

Regardless of income, almost anyone can become wealthy by correcting wasteful spending habits and saving their money. You probably buy many things out of habit without ever really thinking about them. For instance, spending three dollars each workday on a fancy coffee, another two bucks at the soda or snack machine, and then ten dollars at lunch has become a ritual for many Americans. On the surface these small purchases don't seem like a big spending problem, but it is a perfect example of brainless buying. None of these day-to-day costs are necessary, and the pleasures derived from sodas, snacks, lunches, and fancy coffees have a very short shelf life. That's fifteen dollars each workday, and you have nothing to show for it except a thinner wallet and a wider waist.

If you don't think about the desire, the need, the cost, and the reward of your purchases, you are a brainless buyer and you will never be financially secure.

THE *EFFING SOLUTION: BRAINY BUYING

The first step in becoming a brainy buyer is to track your day-to-day expenditures. Buy

It *Effing Figures

Brainless Buying

Let's assume you spend $15 stupidly each day on coffee, lunch, snacks, and sodas while at work. That's $75 each week; $300 each month. In a high-interest savings account with a 6.5 percent interest rate compounded daily, let's see what you could have had:

1 Year = $4,030
5 Years = $21,271
10 Years = $51,143
20 Years = $148,528
40 Years = $692,357

After forty years, your monthly contributions would have totaled $144,300, but the interest gained would total a whopping $540,857! Coffee, snacks, sodas, and lunch will never taste that good.

a bookkeeping record and write down all of your daily purchases, right down to the penny. Include all the tips you leave at restaurants and extraneous expenses. Total your expenses at the end of each day and at the end of each week. By keeping a record of your spending, you will automatically start spending less.

Think hard before you buy. Examine the motivations behind all of your daily purchases. Some experts even recommend writing the motivation behind the purchases in the bookkeeping record along with the cost. This often provides valuable psychological information about your spending habits. Are you buying on impulse? Are you buying to fill an emotional void? Are you buying because of poor planning or laziness? How strong is the desire for the purchase, and how strong is the need? What will the value of your purchase be tomorrow, next week, or next year? Ask yourself all of these questions before you pay for anything. If the value of your purchase perishes quickly, it is a brainless buy. If you are visiting the vending machine because you are bored at work, it is a brainless buy. If you are going out to eat lunch at a restaurant because you forgot to pack a lunch, it is a brainless buy. You work hard for your money, and you should think hard before you spend it.

Top Ten Brainless Buys

1. Anything you see at the checkout counter
2. Single-serving snacks
3. Expensive coffee
4. Alcohol at restaurants and bars
5. Disposable paper goods; expensive toilet paper
6. Designer clothes and accessories
7. High-end beauty products
8. Name-brand medicines
9. Valet parking
10. Brand-new technology

The #5 *Effing Problem:
"No Fun" Finances

Monopoly is the bestselling board game in U.S. history and the most played board game in the world. Since 1935 more than 750 million ordinary people have bought and sold properties, built hotels, owned railroads, electric companies, and water-works. With the roll of the dice, even children learn how to amass fortunes, orchestrate the financial destruction of their competitors, and land a few friends in jail. Given the enormous success of Monopoly and the universal desire for financial secu-rity, it is surprising that so few adults find making money fun. And that's one big reason why most Americans with Boardwalk dreams are still living on Baltic Avenue.

If you fail to find enjoyment in making money and continue to dread your finances, you will never be able to build wealth. With more than 6 million millionaires living in the U.S., there are obviously a lot of people who find making money very enjoy-able. You can, too, but let's first examine the three main reasons why you may not find finances interesting.

You are financially illiterate. Despite the key role money plays in society, most Americans have had no formal financial educa-tion, and you probably have not educated yourself. On a 2004 financial literacy quiz administered by Bankrate.com, only 10 percent of U.S. adults earned an "A" grade, while 35 percent earned an "F." More than one-third of the United States is fail-ing in financial literacy! Overall, the United States earned a pathetic "D." The quiz also revealed that there is a significant gap between financial knowledge and action. While 93 percent of U.S. consumers know that paying bills on time consistently can help avoid penalties and other fees, only 80 percent actually do so. Combine ignorance with inaction and you have the makings of a financial disaster. There were more than one million personal bankruptcies filed in 2008 alone. The average amount of debt owed at the time of bankruptcy filing has also skyrocketed. In these difficult times, nobody can afford to be ignorant about their finances.

True *Effing Fact

Only seven states in the United States require students to take a personal finance exam to graduate high school, and only seventeen states require students to take an economics course.
(*Source:* Council for Economic Education)

You don't relate to money. Some people, especially creative and charitable types, simply do not relate to moneymaking on a personal level. This is the familiar "money is not everything" crowd. It is true—money is meaningless for a few very important things, like loving your children and your faith. But money is very important for a lot of very important things—like housing, food, clothing, education, and recreation. And in these situations where money is very important, it is almost all-important. So it is time for a reality check: the truth is, there would be no starving artists if they all cultivated a relationship with money.

This aversion to making money is only part of the financial relationship problem, however. The digital revolution has also physically and psychologically disconnected you from your finances, making it more difficult to relate to your money. Cash used to be king, but now that king is dead. With direct deposit you rarely see the money you are earning, and with debit cards and credit cards, you rarely see the money you are spending. Sure, you check your statements, but numbers are abstract and difficult to conceptualize—just try thinking about the 2009 national debt: $11.5 trillion. Because the physical and psychological relationship with money has been severed, your bank balances have about the same psychological significance as a high score on Donkey Kong.

You have a bias against being wealthy. You might have a strong bias against wealthy people and not even know it. These unconscious biases are usually manifested as feelings of resentment or envy about someone else's financial success. Wealthy people are often condemned and criticized as being rich snobs, greedy SOBs, gold diggers, and penny-pinchers. These biases are usually baseless. In most cases it takes a lot of effort and integrity to become rich and maintain wealth. These biases may be limited to your subconscious, but they actually prevent you from becoming financially successful. After all, how can you ever become rich if your subversive subconscious despises the rich? It is your internal enemy at work.

THE *EFFING SOLUTION: FUN FINANCES

Unfortunately, saving will never be as much fun as spending. But you can have some fun with your finances and make money more interesting by following a few simple steps:

Simplify your finances. Don't be overdiversified to the point where you no longer can keep track of your finances. It is better to be the master of a few accounts than be a slave to many. Eliminate credit cards you don't frequently use, and pay off your balances.

Cut the confusion. Improve your financial literacy by reading books, attending seminars, and speaking with financial advisors. The website www.practicalmoneyskills.com can really boost your financial knowledge. This site is offered by Visa, but it does a good job at promoting financial literacy for everyone. The site is full of fun and interesting ways to learn about personal finances. In the games section, you can play "Financial Football," test your money skills with the "Get Out of Debt Quiz Show," or hit the highway on the "Road Trip to Savings." The U.S. Congress established the Financial Literacy and Education Commission in 2003. On the organization's website, www.mymoney.gov, you can find easy-to-understand information on various financial topics, including home budgeting, financial planning, debt, and saving for retirement. The U.S. Treasury established the Office of Financial Education in 2002 (www.treas.gov/financialeducation), and it also is a great source of basic financial information.

Do what you love. That might seem like an overly simplistic recommendation, but it is much easier than you think. Let's say you love to ski. You are an office worker at a job you hate because the salary allows you to ski on the weekends. Well, ski resorts have offices, too. So do ski manufacturers, skiing retailers, and tour operators. It is extremely important to feel satisfied in your employment. Finding a job you have a passion for will make you more productive and more creative. You will also be more likely to work overtime and holidays for extra money. If you love your occupation, those extra hours and extra efforts will mean extra income and satisfaction.

Reconnect with cash. Try paying for most purchases with cash. It may be inconvenient, but it is the most effective way to confront your spending habits.

Stop criticizing wealthy people. Overcome your bias against wealthy people.

Track your spending. Record everything you buy.

Increase your earnings. Get creative about earning some extra cash. Sell crafts or turn one of your favorite hobbies into extra cash—or even a full-time job. Teach a night class in something you excel at. Buy and sell items on eBay. Have a garage sale or sell old clothes. If you are a professional, do some consulting work on the side or write articles for trade magazines. Start your own business or develop your own product. Remember: sometimes small ideas can make big money.

True *Effing Fact

In 1943 U.S. Navy engineer Richard James was working in his home laboratory when he accidentally knocked a spring off a shelf and watched it step down onto books, then to the table, then to the floor. The Slinky was born. To date, more than 400 million Slinkys have been sold worldwide.

THE #6 *EFFING PROBLEM:
THE SUCKER SYNDROME

P. T. Barnum once said there is a sucker born every minute, and today there are more fraudsters and hucksters than ever before. Deception has gone digital, and online scam artists are just a few clicks away from stealing your money and your identity. Everyone has been duped before, and nobody is immune from being duped again. Yet despite the countless ways people are deceived, exploited, and betrayed every day, there has been surprisingly little scholarly research in what actually makes people gullible.

The Sucker Syndrome

Signs you might be gullible:

1. You get involved with get-rich-quick schemes.
2. You are often the butt of jokes.
3. You have difficulty saying no.
4. You purchase under pressure from salespeople and telemarketers.
5. You have been repeatedly betrayed by people you thought were friends.
6. You have a lot of self-doubt.
7. You have been criticized for being too trusting.

Gullibility appears to be somewhat dependent on education. People with higher levels of education tend to be less gullible, or at least a bit more cynical. Psychological factors play a strong role in gullibility, too. Negative belief systems like having low self-esteem and high self-doubt can cause people to turn their backs on intuition and common sense with disturbing regularity. But gullibility also seems to be dependent on the situation, and even the sharpest sense of reason can be dulled by desperate circumstances.

Professional scam artists are not the only ones trying to dupe you out of money. Car mechanics, retail clerks, used car salesmen, doctors, even charity fund-raisers are all masters at "up-selling" their wares. As a result of clever sales tactics, millions of Americans buy things they don't want or need, purchase useless warranties, and subscribe to unnecessary services. Anytime you spend more money than you should or give money to someone you shouldn't, you are a victim of the sucker syndrome.

The *Effing Solution: Deception Detection

Very few people are motivated by altruism, so it is best to develop a healthy dose of skepticism. Since you are most likely to get duped about something you know little about, it is also a great idea to educate yourself as much as possible before making any big purchases. Of course, if you have been duped a lot in the past, make sure you learn from your mistakes. With nearly every financial transaction, there is a loser and a winner. If you follow these eight tips, you will come out a winner most of the time:

1. Avoid acting on impulse.
2. Avoid acting on ignorance. Don't assume the other party knows more than you do or has the best intentions.
3. Avoid acting when pressured or rushed.
4. Instead of suppressing your doubts, amplify them.
5. Don't let pride or embarrassment get in the way of saying no.
6. Don't fall for flattery or improbable testimonials.
7. Always be suspicious of unsolicited financial services and loans.
8. Seek the advice of people you trust.

BEWARE! Scam artists also follow the headlines. Quick solutions for home foreclosure, bankruptcy, credit repair, and low-cost health insurance should be considered with extreme suspicion. A lot of these industries are unregulated, and even if there is regulation, it is easy to bend the rules. Here is a list of the biggest sucker syndrome swindles:

Foreclosure Prevention Services. Foreclosure prevention scam artists will ask you for an up-front fee to save your home. Sometimes they will even ask you to sign over the deed to your house. Run away from these cons as fast as you can! Experts recommend contacting your lender directly. You can also speak to an approved housing counselor from the Department of Housing and Urban

Development (HUD). For urgent housing needs or to find a HUD-approved housing counselor, call the Homeowners HOPE Hotline (888) 995-HOPE, or visit www.makinghome affordable.com.

Credit Repair. Complaints against credit repair companies have increased dramatically, according to statistics collected by the Better Business Bureau (BBB). These companies promise to fix your credit and raise your credit score for a large up-front fee. Before you sign up for credit assistance with one of these companies, review their history on the Better Business Bureau website: www.bbb.org. The National Foundation for Credit Counseling also provides low-cost or free credit counseling, as well as counseling for housing and bankruptcy (see www.nfcc.org).

Discount Health Insurance Cards. With 47 million uninsured Americans, the need for low-cost health coverage is greater than ever before. Discount healthcare programs are springing up around the country, and discount card scams are spreading like the plague. For a monthly fee, these companies offer discounts on a variety of dubious medical procedures. Many of these health discounters are legitimate, but others are flat-out fraudulent. The Consumer Health Alliance offers tips on how to find a legitimate plan that will work for you.

Work-at-home Scams. The lure of earning big money at home is almost impossible to resist. "Earn Thousands of Dollars Each Month!" these ads exclaim, but they never deliver on their promises. These "opportunities" often cost you money and a lot of time, according to the Federal Trade Commission. Sometimes work-at-home scams will require the purchase of a starter kit, or you may be asked to buy inventory for sale. Common work-at-home scams include medical billing, envelope stuffing, assembly of products or crafts, and Internet sales.

Extended Warranties. Retailers and auto dealers love pushing extended warranties, and with good reason—they are very profitable. In some cases, like consumer electronics, the warranty sales make up the bulk of the store profits. According to Consumer Reports, extended warranties are a big financial mistake for almost every product they research, from home appliances and electronics to new cars. The risk of needing a repair on a new product is too low, and the cost of extended warranties is too high. Plus, most manufacturers offer a standard one-year warranty, and some credit card companies will extend this. Don't buy into the sales scare tactics! Don't buy the warranty.

Pump-and-dump Stock Scams. These "pump-and-dump" stock campaigns used to come from cold-calling boiler room stock traders, but now they often show up in your e-mail box. In fact, some estimate that pump-and-dump e-mails make up 15 percent of all spam e-mail. In a pump-and-dump stock scam, a company that owns a stock will artificially inflate the price with false or misleading statements. This attracts gullible investors, who are duped into pumping extra cash into the stock. The company will then sell—or dump—all of its stock at the inflated price and send its value plummeting. The Securities and Exchange Commission offers tips on how to avoid these pump-and-dump scams (see www.sec.gov).

Foreign Exchange Investment Scams. Investments in foreign currencies are often advertised as low-risk, high-yield opportunities, but nothing could be further from the truth. Foreign exchange investment scam artists will ask for a large amount of money to secure the investment in the foreign currency. In most cases, you never see the money again. You must investigate before you invest with anyone.

Investment Seminars. Attending financial advice seminars can be extraordinarily helpful. But there are a lot of scammers in this area, too. Beware of seminars where attendees are pressured to sign up immediately, or the opportunity will be missed. Guarantees of high profits, improbable testimonials, and seductive property investments are also major red flags. Sleep on it, think about it, and investigate the company. When attending any investment seminar, never sign on-site.

Advanced Fee Loan Scams. Advanced fee loan scammers prey on people who are the most financially vulnerable in our society. Sometimes they target minority groups or veterans. They often promise a guaranteed loan approval or a line of credit, regardless of your credit history in exchange for an up-front fee. Once the up-front fee is submitted, the applicant is often told that they did not qualify for the loan but may be eligible for a different loan—for an additional fee.

Nigerian Scams. These are often called Nigerian 419 scams or Nigerian e-mail scams. In the most familiar e-mail scheme, a Nigerian national or aristocrat pleads for your assistance in recovering a large sum of money. They ask you to wire transfer a small sum of money, and in return they promise you a share of the financial windfall. Your money disappears. In more elaborate scams, Nigerians will bid on legitimate auction items, win the bid, and send a bogus check. You deposit the check, and before you realize the check is bogus, they have acquired your banking information. These kinds of scams are not limited to Nigeria, and needless to say, most Nigerians are not Internet scam artists.

THE #7 *EFFING PROBLEM: SUNK COST FALLACY

Nobody enjoys losing money or making a poor investment. Economists use the term "sunk cost" for these past expenses or efforts that can never be recovered. It could be a losing stock, an automobile in constant need of repairs, a business failing, or a home that has become a money pit. Behavioral economic studies suggest that something funny happens when you consider these sunk costs—you don't act rationally.

Let's use a plane ticket as a dramatic example. You purchase a nonrefundable round-trip plane ticket for $500. After you make the purchase, you see a television news report about the airline's shoddy safety record and poor maintenance standards. What do you do? Do you take your trip or not? If you had not already spent the money, you would probably just book a seat on another airline. That seems rational enough. But since you already spent the $500, it changes your decision, and you are much more likely to get on that airplane. This is an irrational decision, because the $500 is a sunk cost; it is irrecoverable. The money you spent should not influence your decision to fly or not to fly, because it has nothing to do with your main concern: do you want to fly on a potentially unsafe aircraft? Not flying on this airline and losing your money is the most rational decision in this case.

In personal finance, when people are presented with a sunk cost, instead of throwing in the towel, they continue to fund it. The irrational decision to pursue these lost causes is called a "sunk cost fallacy." It is the "I can't stop now" mentality. People are reluctant to accept financial loss. They are what economists call "loss averse." They also become overly optimistic about an eventual payoff of the sunk cost. The combination of loss aversion and irrational optimism may cause you to throw good money after bad and pour more money into a sunk cost, all the while banking on an eventual turnaround. In many instances, abandoning your sunk cost is the most rational and most profitable thing to do.

THE *EFFING SOLUTION:
OPPORTUNITY COSTS

Identify all of the sunk costs in your life and consider abandoning them or modifying your goals. This is particularly challenging because nobody can predict the future, and in rare cases, sunk costs can suddenly turn around and pay off. Additionally, identifying a sunk cost often involves admitting a mistake or

failure. But give all your possible sunk costs careful consideration, because if your failings are not recognized, they will only
grow larger. Be prepared. Changing your decision-making
behavior can be very difficult, and giving up on a sunk cost often
involves giving up dreams and desires.

You also must learn how to consider what economists call
"opportunity costs." Opportunity costs are the shadow prices
that follow every one of your financial
decisions. They are the assumed financial impact of "the next-best option."
Suppose you are about to begin your
second year of law school when you
decide you no longer want to become a
lawyer and would rather become a
florist. The sunk cost is the tuition
money and the time you wasted by
going to law school for one year. Now
let's take a look at the opportunity cost. The opportunity cost is
the one year of law school tuition that you could have saved, plus
the income you could have earned as a florist, plus the time lost
becoming an experienced florist. Remember, the true cost of
something is not only the price tag, but the cost of what you are
giving up to get it.

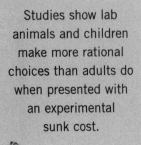

True *Effing Fact

Studies show lab
animals and children
make more rational
choices than adults do
when presented with
an experimental
sunk cost.

Unlike sunk costs, opportunity costs can be forward-looking,
and that makes them a powerful weapon in avoiding some major
financial mistakes. Let's use the law school example again. You
fall victim to the sunk cost fallacy and continue law school. The

opportunity cost of continuing your studies and obtaining a law degree would be the three years of tuition money that could be saved in a high-interest savings account, plus the three years of lost wages you could earn as a florist, plus three years of lost flower shop experience. It's important to mention that many law students acquire a lot of credit card debt while in school, too. Of course, having a law degree is very valuable—if you want to become a lawyer. But it is a colossal financial mistake if you want to become a florist. Always look for your sunk costs and compare them to your opportunity costs.

Here are some tips that can keep sunk costs from sinking you:

Got that Sinking Feeling?

Keep the following in mind when making major financial decisions:

1. Consider the sunk cost and compare it to the opportunity cost.
2. Don't become too attached to your effort. Even good ideas fail.
3. Don't own the failure; own the decision to stay or move on.
4. Do not make decisions for the future based on past investments.
5. Adopt a "fresh start" philosophy.
6. Act today for tomorrow.
7. Keep your plans fluid. Success requires adaptability.
8. Seek the advice of people who are not emotionally invested in the possible sunk cost.

THE #8 *EFFING PROBLEM: DUMB DEBT

In 2006 the United States Census Bureau estimated that there were nearly 1.5 billion credit cards in the United States. If you stacked all those credit cards on top of each other, it would create a tower of plastic that would stretch seventy miles into space! The number of Americans with credit cards is expected to jump to 181 million in the year 2010. Today the average U.S. consumer has thirteen credit obligations on record at a credit bureau, nine of which are credit cards. When used properly, credit cards can improve your credit score and provide a convenient and immediate source of purchasing power. But millions of Americans use credit cards improperly, and that's when they become financially dangerous. The average interest rate on a consumer credit card is about 15 percent, and credit card companies charge hefty penalties for late payments. Industry experts estimate that about 70 percent of credit card revenue comes from the collection of interest charges and late fees. Dumb debt is big business.

> **True *Effing Fact**
>
> If you charged a $2,000 vacation on a credit card with a 15 percent APR and made minimum monthly payments of $25, it would take ninety-three months to pay it off. That's nearly eight years and about $1,085 in interest alone!

Credit card purchases are not always dumb debt, and they are not the only source of dumb debt. Buying a house you cannot afford and buying an expensive car are two other important sources of dumb debt. There is also such a thing as "smart debt" —or perhaps it is better described as "less dumb debt." These are debts that can improve your financial situation if you don't borrow too much, get a low interest rate, and consistently make payments. Student loans and home mortgages often fall into this category. Knowing which of your debts are dumb and which are smart is critical to getting out of debt as soon as possible.

THE *EFFING SOLUTION: PAY DOWN DEBT

The first step to paying down your debt is to stop accumulating it. Establish a budget and make sure you are sticking to it. Cut back on your spending, evaluate your opportunity costs, and eliminate any sunk costs. Review your assets, including savings accounts and retirement accounts—you might need to liquidate them to pay off your dumb debt.

1. Examine all of your debts and separate your smart debt from your dumb debt.

2. Speak to your creditors about lowering your current interest rate.

3. Identify your dumbest debt. This is usually the credit card or consumer loan with the highest interest rate.

4. Aggressively pay as much as possible each month on your dumbest debt obligation. If you can pay off the entire balance, do it. If you cannot, you must *always* pay more than the minimum on your highest interest debt.

5. While you are paying down your dumbest debt, continue to make the minimum payments on all of your other credit obligations, including the smart debt. Remember, if you don't pay the minimum payment on smart debt, it can turn into dumb debt.

6. You might need to use your savings account or emergency fund. In general, if your savings or emergency account is not earning more than 20 percent, it should be sacrificed to pay off high-interest debts.

7. Consolidate payments to the lowest possible interest rate. If you have available balance on a lower-interest credit card, consider transferring your balances from higher-interest credit cards. This is called "snowballing."

8. Pay more than the minimum. This applies only to dumb debt, and it may not be the best advice to pay down smart debt instead of saving for retirement or college.

9. When your highest interest rate debt is paid off, move on to the credit obligation with the next highest interest rate.

10. Do not use a home equity loan to pay off your outstanding credit card debt. Credit card debt is an unsecured debt, meaning if you default, the creditor cannot come after your home. But home mortgages are secured debt, and if you default on payments, the lender can foreclose on your home.

Get help before it becomes too late. American Consumer Credit Counseling (ACCC) is a nonprofit 501(c)(3) organization that offers credit counseling and other financial services. The ACCC website, www.consumercredit.com, has many useful tools like a credit card interest calculator, debt payoff calculator, college funding calculator, and even a brown-bag lunch calculator. The National Foundation for Credit Counseling (NFCC) also has a credit card payment calculator on their website, www.nfcc.org, as well as other financial services. Many consumer credit counseling agencies can negotiate with your creditors and lenders, and help arrange a lower monthly payment.

Once you are out of debt, it is important to stay out of debt. Don't live above your means. Don't buy an expensive new car. Live in a modest home. Don't use credit cards to pay for extravagant vacations or everyday purchases like groceries, drinks, and meals at restaurants. Also avoid credit cards that offer rewards. If you are a prudent shopper, reward cards can pay off, but they usually come with higher interest rates and will cost you more money in the long run.

THE #9 *EFFING PROBLEM: LIVING BEYOND YOUR MEANS

The economic downturn and the housing crisis revealed just how many people in the United States have been living beyond their means. In 2008 there was a record loss of personal wealth— more than $11 trillion—and personal bankruptcy filings and foreclosures hit epidemic proportions. It seems our "keeping up with the Joneses" mentality finally caught up to us. We have become a nation of hyperconsumers. Most Americans are spending more than they should, and many are spending more than they are earning. Unfortunately, the biggest overspenders are those who can least afford it. According to statistics from the Department of Commerce, households in the lowest income bracket spend nearly double their income, and middle-income households spend more than three-quarters of their total income. To build your net worth, you must spend much less than you earn. It is that simple.

Signs You Might Be Living Above Your Means

1. You have a hard time making the minimum payments on your credit cards.
2. Your credit card balances are rising or are maxed out.
3. You have no savings or are tapping into savings to pay your bills.
4. You have a credit score below 600.
5. You are living paycheck to paycheck.
6. You don't know how much debt you actually have.

THE *EFFING SOLUTION: GET OUT OF "JONESTOWN"

There are really only two reliable ways of building wealth: increasing your earnings or decreasing your spending. Of course, the quickest way to build wealth is to do both. Establishing a budget, curtailing your expenses, and learning how to relate to money will help you do that. But it will be much easier if you stop trying to keep up with the Joneses. It might even be bad for your health. A 2009 study published in the journal *Social Science and Medicine* found people who envied the successes of their neighbors and friends were more likely to suffer from ulcers, diabetes, high blood pressure, and heart disease. You must escape from Jonestown.

Redefine richness. Most people do not consider themselves "rich" no matter how much money they have. A 2003 Gallup poll found that only 2 percent of people described themselves as rich, which means 98 percent of us felt unrich. But compared to most of the world, the average American is indeed very rich. So why don't you feel wealthy? Wealth is relative. Material possessions do not make people happy for long, and the pleasure they do create often sours over time—especially if the possessions are still being paid for. Redefine what you mean by wealth. You don't have to celebrate frugality, but do celebrate fiscal responsibility and healthy savings. Real wealth is being debt free, having growing investments, being able to fund the dreams of your children, and having plenty of money for retirement or perhaps an early retirement.

> True *Effing* Fact
>
> The saying "keeping up with the Joneses" originated as the title to a comic strip. Cartoonist Arthur R. Momand created the strip, which debuted in 1916 and ran in American newspapers for twenty-eight years. The Joneses were the neighbors of the main characters.

Recognize needless necessities. In 1990 only an elite few owned a cell phone, and nobody had Internet service. Heck, the Internet itself wasn't even available until the mid-1990s. But today most people would have a hard time living without these "necessities." Having cable television and having two cars in every household has become equally important to our way of life. However, for some people, these can be seen as "needless necessities," simple luxuries that are hard to live without. It's important to note that a person's notion of luxury and necessity is never fixed. A recent poll by the Pew Research Center reports that today 33 percent of Americans consider cable television a necessity, but only about half of that (17 percent) thought so back in 1996.

Not long ago, only wealthy people hired maids or cleaning services, but now many of your neighbors probably do. Take a look at your necessities and decide if they are, in fact, luxuries. If they are a luxury you can do without, consider getting rid of them. Before you purchase any big-ticket item, decide if it is one of these needless necessities. Other items moving up the needless necessity list include large-screen, high-definition television sets, cell phones for every child, computers and televisions in every room, and expensive appliances in every kitchen.

Homegrown?

Single-family homes have grown:

In 1950, an average-sized home was 983 square feet.
In 1970, an average-sized home was 1,500 square feet.
In 2005, an average-sized home was 2,434 square ft.
And homes are still getting bigger! Forty percent of homes being built today have four or more bedrooms.

(*Source:* National Association of Home Builders)

Get over it. You're not going to get rich quick. Achieving financial security and building wealth can take a long time, especially if you are already in debt. Don't look for shortcuts, and don't expect to see results immediately. Increased earning, decreased spending, and consistent saving is a slow but sure road to financial freedom. Let the Joneses spend their way into bankruptcy, foreclosure, and an uncertain future.

Stop pushing the bucks. Assume personal responsibility for your financial failures and successes. When it comes to the spending habits of your neighbors and friends, MYOB.

THE #10 *EFFING PROBLEM: DUMB INVESTING

Individual investors in the stock market often fall victim to fad investments and hot stock picks. The dot-com bubble burst on March 10, 2000, and technology companies lost a market value of $5 trillion within two years. Ordinary people saw their investment and retirement accounts evaporate. Others make the common mistake of putting too much money in high-risk stocks or simply fail to diversify their portfolio. But even smart investors and professionals can be burned by bad investments. Warren Buffet lost more than $8 billion in the stock market in 2008 and saw the value of his company, Berkshire Hathaway, lose $11.5 billion in the same year. Buffet was remarkably blunt about the company's financial performance in his chairman's letter: "During 2008 I did some dumb things in investments," he wrote.

Poor investments are certainly not limited to Wall Street. People pour their hard-earned money into pyramid schemes, investment properties, time-shares, and new cars, only to see the value of these investments depreciate or disappear.

THE *EFFING SOLUTION: "SEVEN DEADLY SINS" OF PERSONAL INVESTING

1. **Buying a new car:** All new cars depreciate at different speeds depending on model popularity and reliability. On average, a new car depreciates at 15–20 percent of its value each year for the first few years. Roughly 40 percent of the car's initial value is lost in the first three years. Would you buy a stock that depreciated as quickly? Over years 3–6, the car loses only 25 percent of its value. Sam Walton, the founder of Walmart, drove his old pickup

truck until the day he died. A better financial move is to buy a "nearly new" car, a few years old with low mileage. It will give you that new car feeling, you will pay much less money up front, and lose much less over time.

2. **Buying a house that is too big:** Do not buy a home that is more than three times your annual income. Experts recommend spending 2.5–3 times your annual income on a new home. The mortgage should be manageable, and a larger mortgage will likely put you in the financial danger zone. Plus, larger homes have higher taxes and much higher utility bills.

3. **Banking on bubbles:** Throughout history, financial bubbles have blown up and burst. It is true that the dot-com bubble of 1998–2001 created some millionaires, and some savvy home investors made a lot of money during the housing bubble of 2000–2005. But millions of Americans lost trillions of dollars when both bubbles burst. Financial and real estate insiders fueled the earliest stages of these bubbles, when they were most profitable and secure. By the time most ordinary folks jumped in, the bubbles were ready to burst.

4. **Investing emotionally:** Don't invest your money on stocks or get-rich-quick schemes based on greed, or out of fear that you will miss out on an opportunity.

5. **Trying to time the market:** The stock market acts like a terrible two-year-old at times, and a troubled teenager at

others. It is prone to tantrums, mood swings, and irra-
tionality. With all of the ups and downs, a diversified
portfolio will still net you a 10 percent annual return at
ten years and twenty years. Don't panic in bad times and
trade too often. In most cases, the more you trade your
holdings, the more money you lose.

6. **Complicating your finances:** Keep your financial picture
simple. Your financial portfolio should minimize your risk
and maximize your long-term growth. You must be able
to understand and track your investments, and make
occasional adjustments.

7. **Buying the product, not the stock:** Got your eye on a
trendy purchase? Save your money and investigate the
stock instead.

4 Your *Effing Job

THE #1 *EFFING PROBLEM: YOU DON'T LIKE YOUR JOB

How much do you like your job? Several recent surveys suggest that more than half of all U.S. employees are not satisfied with their current employment, and roughly 40 percent would change careers if given the opportunity. But with a struggling economy and an anemic job market, changing careers is not a realistic option for a lot of people. As a result, many are working in distasteful and dissatisfying jobs for longer periods of time.

There are several competing theories about what makes a job satisfying or unsatisfying. According to what is called the "disposition theory," some people have personalities that make them much more likely to find satisfaction at work, regardless of the job they are performing. Of course, there are other people who are prone to being dissatisfied at work. There is some evidence to support the disposition theory. Some studies have shown that a person's job satisfaction remains relatively constant throughout their entire working career, and identical twins with different jobs usually report a similar degree of job satisfaction. But other theories have suggested that the nature of the job is the most important factor. The "affect theory" argues that job satisfaction arises when job experience meets job expectations, and dissatisfaction results if there is a discrepancy. The "job characteristics" model argues that there are five core job characteristics that contribute most to work satisfaction, namely: skill variety, task significance, task identity, autonomy, and feedback. None of the theories are mutually exclusive, and it is likely that several theories play a role in job satisfaction. However, jobs that are rated as unsatisfying do share some common characteristics: there is usually little autonomy, little sense of control, little recognition, and job tasks seem insignificant.

It *Effing Figures

> The average American worker will have about eleven jobs between ages 18 and 42.
> (*Source:* Bureau of Labor Statistics)

THE *EFFING SOLUTION: HOW TO GET SOME JOB SATISFACTION

If you are unhappy in your current job, you have four basic choices: make your current job more satisfying, change careers, pursue your dream job, or don't work at all. Since unemployment is not a practical choice for most people, let's start with the easiest and least appealing option: how to make your unsatisfying job more satisfying.

Between the ages of eighteen and fifty-five, the average American worker will spend more than eight entire years at work. Your job fulfillment has a large impact on your self-esteem. If you do not feel good about your job, it is very hard to feel good about yourself. So it is essential that you try to make your work more fulfilling. Research has shown that employees are most dissatisfied when they have little control, little significance, and little feedback. Concentrating on improving these three aspects of your current job can dramatically improve your on-the-job satisfaction. Carefully suggest ways to improve the work atmosphere to your manager or superior. Ask your superior for more responsibility and volunteer to take on more challenging tasks. Perhaps you can spearhead a pet project or organize a club or a charity benefit. Do something enterprising, but make it important. The new task must matter to you and the company. By doing this you will gain some control and increase the significance of your job. And don't forget to ask for feedback from your superiors and coworkers. Criticism hones your skills, and the easiest way to get praise is to ask for it.

Famous Midlife Career Changers

President Ronald Reagan was an actor. Arnold Schwarzenegger is an action hero turned state governor. Martha Stewart was a stockbroker before becoming a television host and lifestyle magnate. Mohandas Gandhi was a lawyer before becoming the political and spiritual leader of the Indian independence movement. The famous

Italian tenor Andrea Bocelli was also a lawyer, but has since sold 60 million albums worldwide.

If you are completely dissatisfied with your current job, it may be time to consider a career change. It is never too late to change careers, and many retirees find enormous gratification in pursuing a second career. But don't quit your current job—stay employed! You will be much more confident and marketable if you already have a job. If you are not sure what second career suits your personality, you can find free career personality assessments online at websites like CareerBuilder.com and Monster.com. It is important to do as much research as possible into your next career and get some definitive experience. Doing an internship or shadowing a professional in the field is an effective, low-cost way to gain some experience and make some contacts. Develop new skills that will make you more marketable to potential employers, and start rewriting your résumé. Remember, sometimes a hobby can be turned into a side career and ultimately into a full-time career.

Now, let's discuss your dream job. What did you want to become when you were younger, and why did you give it up? That might sound like a silly question, but answering it today is more important than it was back in kindergarten. Did you want to become an astronaut, a firefighter, a NASCAR driver, a movie star, or perhaps a talk show host? So why didn't you become that? The answer for most people can be summed up in one word:

reality. By nature children are unrealistic. They have tea parties with imaginary friends. They never have to put food on the table or pay a bill. But for adults, impracticality is seen as immature and fanciful. There are some large flaws in this kind of thinking. For one thing, most young children are happy, while many adults are not. Plus, there are people who actually earn a living as astronauts, firefighters, NASCAR drivers, movie stars, and talk show hosts. So let's re-suspend reality for a moment. What do you really want to be?

If you are thinking there are too many dreamers and not enough jobs, you are right. After all, it is impossible for everyone to have their dream job. We'd have way too many rock stars and far too few plumbers. But one big thing is working in your favor: most people have given up on landing their dream job and they are never going to try. So you can live your dreams—you might even encounter less competition than you think. Here are some steps that can help you land that dream job.

True *Effing Fact

According to a 2007 survey from CareerBuilder.com, more than four out of five American workers do not have their "dream job."

1. **Plan it out on paper:** Writing things down will help you think more clearly and rationally. Write down what you want to do and your qualifications. Then describe your motivation and what you expect to get from the job. Is it fame? Fortune? Flexibility? More time with your family?

Fun? List what you would need to do to land that dream job. You might have to go back to school or learn new skills. Make sure the average salary of your dream job can accommodate your current lifestyle. If not, are you willing to make the necessary lifestyle adjustments?

2. **Nibble before you bite, and chew before you swallow:** Suddenly quitting your current job to pursue your dream job would be disastrous. First you must find out as much as you can about your dream job. Do an internship, shadow someone while you are on vacation, volunteer at night or on weekends, and use your social network to get advice from people who currently have your dream job. This exploration phase usually leads to valuable contacts. Arrange meetings with people in the field you are trying to break into. You will be surprised how many people are willing to offer free career advice. In your conversations, don't forget to ask about the downside of your dream job. Inquire about the lifestyle and other demands. Is there anything they hate about the job? You must get as much real data as possible.

3. **Beef up your résumé:** Your résumé should reflect your passion for the new field and list related experiences. This is not a weekend task. For some people strengthening a résumé may take months or even years. If you have no experience, you must get some, and that can take a while.

4. **Go for it**: Madonna came to New York as a dancer with
$35 in her pocket. Sylvester Stallone was a struggling
actor working at a deli counter when he wrote the screen-
play to *Rocky*. Funny man and political satirist Stephen
Colbert made a brief but spirited run for the U.S.
presidency, authored a number-one bestselling book,
and released a popular Christmas album. A new species
of spider, a Ben & Jerry's ice cream flavor, and a treadmill
on the International Space Station have all been named
for Colbert. Plus, he has won a Peabody Award and a few
Emmy Awards along the way! You can live the dream or
love the dream. Colbert does both. Go for it—and have
some fun.

Your dream job does not have to be glamorous or sensational.
You don't have to change the world. But by becoming happier at
work, you will be changing *your* world, which is really all that
matters.

THE #2 *EFFING PROBLEM:
TIME-WASTING ACTIVITIES (TWAs)

A survey conducted by AOL and Salary.com in 2005 estimated that the average employee spends more than two hours
each workday wasting time—and that's not counting lunch.
Each year U.S. businesses lose $759 billion in lost productivity
due to time-wasting activities (TWAs). Using the Internet for

personal purposes is by far the most commonly abused TWA in the workplace today. Because Internet use is easily concealed and looks similar to actual work, it is a growing problem in corporate America. According to a survey by the International Data Corporation (IDC), between 30–40 percent of all Internet usage during working hours is not business-related, and almost all employees admit to conducting at least some personal business on the company computer. We shop and trade stocks online, chat with friends and family by instant messaging (IM) or e-mail, and we update our Twitter, MySpace, and Facebook profiles on company time. An article in *PC World* magazine even offers a list of "40 Fantastic Time-Wasting Websites" that can help vaporize extra hours from your workday. And though few people admit to accessing pornography at work, SexTracker.com claims that 68 percent of all Internet pornography viewing occurs during regular business hours.

High Price of Cyberslacking

Some experts have suggested that cyberslacking costs American businesses more than $1 billion annually in computer and Internet use.

But the Internet is not the only TWA on the job; there are also coffee and cigarette breaks, two-hour lunches, and lengthy conversations on the telephone or at the watercooler. The most common reasons cited for wasting company time are: not having enough work, unchallenging job assignments, procrastination, and working too many hours for too little pay.

The *Effing Solution: Distraction Detox

Being productive at work is good for the corporate bottom line and good for your mental health. Several studies have shown that increasing your productivity will increase your job satisfaction, and productive employees are happier employees. If you are having a problem remaining focused at work, it might be time for distraction detox.

Identify the reasons why you are wasting time. Some people waste time at work because they hate their boss or they get a thrill out of breaking the corporate rules. But most TWAs do not have any malicious intent. Boredom and procrastination are the most common reasons cited for wasting time. Others feel overworked, underpaid, and entitled to waste some time. Try to correct the problem at its source. If you are bored, ask for more challenging job assignments and take steps to overcome procrastination.

Stop Procrastinating!

Procrastination affects all aspects of life. We avoid going to the doctor, committing to relationships, saving money, and doing our jobs. Here's how to break the habit:

- **Face your fear:** Doing the most formidable task first in the morning can help you feel accomplished for the rest of the day.
- **Stop planning and start doing:** Overplanning is the most common form of procrastination. It is good to plan a little, but then get started. You will have to adjust anyway.
- **Break the task down:** Break large tasks into smaller components.
- **Start small:** Tackle the smallest component of the task first, then move on to larger components.
- **Set a finish line:** Your task needs a definitive end point. You must work toward a preestablished goal. It is extremely important to visualize task completion and see projects through until the end.

By breaking your procrastination habit and asking for more challenging job assignments, your workday will have less room for TWAs, and your managers will appreciate your initiative. If you are being overworked, delegate responsibilities or ask for help. And if you are being underpaid, ask for a raise.

1. **Track your TWAs:** For two days write down all of your TWAs and how much time you waste on them. Be honest. It is also a good idea to jot down the reason for the TWA.

2. **Calculate:** Add up all of the time you spend on nonwork activities while at work. Most people are surprised to learn how many hours they waste. Your goal: cut the TWA time in half.

3. **Make changes:** If examining your TWAs makes you feel a little guilty, it should. Don't sabotage your job with senseless waste. Millions of Americans lose their jobs each year, and millions more are currently unemployed. There are plenty of people willing to do your job for less money. So make some changes.

TWA Prevention Plan

1. **Make a hit list:** Start each morning by creating a to-do list, set goals, and stick to them. Don't allow any TWAs until the list has been completed.

2. **Develop a routine:** If your job consists of predictable tasks each day, get into a routine that excludes TWAs. Set a time when a specific TWA is allowable.

3. **E-mail:** Avoid using your corporate e-mail as your personal e-mail. Give your personal e-mail to friends and resist checking it at work. Don't keep your corporate e-mail open on your computer desktop. Check it every hour or half hour instead. This prevents inefficient multitasking.

4. **Avoid forums, social networking, and chat rooms.**

5. **Make your workspace "transparent":** Keep the projects you are working on visible on your desk. Position your computer in such a way that your coworkers or boss can see your computer screen.

It is normal to waste a little bit of time at work doing personal business, and it might even boost productivity to some extent. At the end of each day you should feel accomplished but not exhausted. A word of caution about company Internet use: most major corporations are now using sophisticated programs to monitor employee e-mails and Internet activity. TWAs are taken very seriously, and firings over Internet abuses are on the increase.

THE #3 *EFFING PROBLEM: YOU HAVE BAD WORK HABITS

We all have coworkers who show up to meetings late and unprepared. Some of them leave early on Fridays, call in sick on Mondays, and take long lunches. Every office has a snob, a slob, a few desk disasters, scatterbrains, and whiners. You know it if you are one of them. These kinds of behaviors hurt productivity, lower office morale, and lower your chances of getting a promotion. Let's take a look at some common bad work habits, and how they actually translate to your coworkers and superiors.

Bad Work Habit Translator

What You Do	What It Says
You are always late for work.	You don't care about your job and have poor time-management skills.
You leave early.	Your professional life is not a priority.

You are always calling in sick.	You are willing to bend the truth, misuse your benefits, and take advantage of coworkers.
You are late for meetings.	You don't care about wasting your coworkers' time and do not manage your own time well.
You miss deadlines.	Your organizational skills are poor, and you are unwilling to put in the extra effort needed to meet your deadlines.
You are constantly multitasking.	You are unfocused and inefficient.
You complain a lot.	You do not value your job, respect your coworkers, or respect your superiors.

THE *EFFING SOLUTION: SEVEN SECRETS OF SMART WORKERS

Anyone can work hard. Even donkeys can work hard. You need to work smart.

This should be the motto of the modern workforce. Today's most effective companies are powered by employees who show initiative and ingenuity. While it is still very important to work hard, working smart is much more important. Take a look around your workplace. Identify the "smart workers" in your office—those who are respected by coworkers and superiors alike—then closely examine their work habits. They probably do things much differently than the rest of your coworkers. Smart workers usually follow these seven secrets of success. You should too.

1. **Smart workers arrive early and leave late.** Getting to the office before your boss is ideal. It gives you some uninterrupted time to organize your workday, and your boss will notice the extra effort. Leaving the office after your boss does is also a smart move. Admittedly, neither may be possible in many cases. But smart workers are usually one of the first employees into the office and one of the last to leave. Smart workers also show up for meetings on time. In fact, they usually show up ten minutes early. Being early to a meeting is a prime opportunity for you to do some relaxed socializing with managers and coworkers. When it comes to business meetings today, if you arrive five minutes early, you are already five minutes too late.

2. **Smart workers don't show up empty-handed.** Come prepared for meetings with all the necessary papers, pens, presentation tools, and data.

3. **Smart workers don't show up empty-headed.** Before leaving the office, prepare work for the following morning. Don't spend half of the morning wondering what you should be working on. Stay engaged in your work by having a mental game plan for each day. During business

meetings always bring your best ideas to the table. Participate in business meetings. It is essential that you read over the meeting agenda beforehand and make sure your ideas are well crafted for discussion.

4. **Smart workers don't multitask, they prioritize.** Being busy does not necessarily mean you are being efficient. You should not be spending the entire day sending rapid-fire e-mail responses. Focus on one task at a time. When the task is completed, move on to the next task. Resist multitasking. It is a highly inefficient habit. Recent research has shown that the brain operates most efficiently when performing one task at a time. By avoiding the multi-tasking trap, you become more efficient and competent at completing the task.

True *Effing Fact

Call it a double-duty delusion. A 2009 Stanford University study found that people who consider themselves exceptional multitaskers were actually the worst at multitasking.

5. **Smart workers are flexible.** Be willing to adjust and compromise to get the job done properly. Keeping your business strategies fluid and open for modification will prevent frustration and help you stay motivated. Ask for feedback from your superiors and learn from honest criticism. Don't gripe if your boss wants something done another way. Just do it.

6. **Smart workers aren't just team players, they are team leaders.** Assume full responsibility for whatever task you are given, no matter how small or seemingly insignificant. Keep everyone informed of your progress, cooperate with your team, and always lead by example.

7. **Smart workers are results oriented.** Have clear goals and expectations for yourself and other members of your corporate team. Success takes sacrifice and requires frequent assessments and adjustments to meet your goals. Commit to achieving results.

THE #4 *EFFING PROBLEM: YOU'RE A SLOB ON THE JOB

Books are judged by their covers in corporate America. A study recently published in the *Intelligence* finds that even after accounting for intelligence, good-looking people are more highly educated than average-looking people, and they make significantly more money. Numerous earlier studies came to similar conclusions. In one study researchers from the University of Pittsburgh used income data and a five-point scale of facial attractiveness to calculate the exact dollar amount of this "beauty bonus." For each point of facial attractiveness, men made $2,600 more in annual income and women earned an extra $2,150. And this study was conducted in 1983! Today each point of physical attractiveness would be worth more than $5,000.

If you are overweight, don't expect a fat paycheck, especially if you are a woman. On average, obese workers make 2.5 percent less on each paycheck than their normal-weight counterparts in the same job. One study from New York University found that as a woman's weight increases, family income decreases and so does her occupational prestige.

It's also important to dress professionally at work. A survey of 150 CEOs and senior executives found that the large major-ity of them believed that inappropriate workplace attire negatively affects productivity, and two-thirds believed that pro-fessional attire plays a strong role in corporate advancement. Another study found that flirty and provocatively dressed women get fewer raises and promotions. Don't forget about your per-sonal hygiene. Having excessive body odor, bad breath, or being unclean or sloppy can also sabotage your career. How you look and smell is a reflection of how you feel, and everybody likes to work with a confident, competent, and inoffensive employee.

It *Effing Figures

Heavy Price

Obese employees cost U.S. businesses more than $45 billion in annual medical costs and lost work.

(*Source:* Conference Board)

THE *EFFING SOLUTION: FROM MESS TO SUCCESS

Dress for success. If you are a boxing coach, the dress code is a little more liberal than it is in the boardroom. But for most corporations, it is usually good advice to dress similarly to your supervisors, or even a bit more conservatively. The old business adage, "Don't dress for the job you have, dress for the job you want," applies under most circumstances.

- **Men:** All of your suits and shirts should be clean and properly fitted. An improperly fitting suit looks sloppier than a more casual outfit that fits. Always avoid wearing loud patterns, thick and garish pinstripes, and novelty ties. Buy a few good pairs of brown and black shoes, as well as identical pairs of black socks, dark blue socks, and brown socks. Buy six pairs of each color; this way you don't have to struggle to find matching socks in the morning. Don't bathe in cologne—it grosses out most of your coworkers, including the women.

- **Women:** Jewelry should be simple, and your makeup and hair should be understated. It is okay to dress stylishly, but avoid fads and never dress provocatively. Provocatively dressed women are not taken seriously in the workplace. All of your outfits should be clean and well pressed. Business suits, skirts, blouses, and jackets are the norm, and they should fit properly or be tailored. Avoid flashy colors or unusual patterns. Your bra and panties should never be visible through your clothing. Shoes should be closed-toe in a style and color that complements your outfit. Don't wear large amounts of perfume or scented skin creams.

Don't Become a Casual Friday Casualty. Casual Friday is not Freaky Friday or Frumpy Friday. It is more appropriately called Business-Casual Friday. Your clothes should be neat, clean, and in good shape. Never wear sweatpants unless you work in a gym. Never wear shorts, flip-flops, or sandals unless you work at the beach. Never wear a halter top unless you are working at Hooters. Women shouldn't show more skin than they would on an ordinary workday.

Disastrous desks. Having a clean desk can improve focus and help you relax at work. But if your desk is too neat, then you are probably spending too much time cleaning and organizing and not enough time working. If your desk is too messy, it will hinder productivity and reflect poorly on your organizational skills. Your desk is an extension of your mind. It should be kept busy but not buried.

Bad breath. Situational bad breath is commonly caused by foods (cheeses, garlic, onions, fish, and meats), alcohol, and cigarettes. Brushing your teeth, flossing, and using mouthwash are usually effective remedies. Chronic bad breath, however, represents a more serious problem and is most often due to odor-producing bacteria inside the mouth. Treating chronic bad breath can be difficult. Mints, gum, and mouthwash only mask the smell. Since most of the odor-producing bacteria grow on the drier back portion of the tongue, many experts recommend using a tongue scraper or a toothbrush to clean it.

True *Effing Fact

There are about 600 different kinds of bacteria in the average mouth.

Chronic bad breath can also be caused by tooth decay and gum disease. Occasionally, persistent bad breath can be a sign of serious medical conditions like liver failure, lung infections, and stomach problems. In all cases of persistent bad breath, a medical and dental evaluation is warranted. Tips for beating bad breath include brushing your teeth and your tongue, gargling with mouthwash, using gum to keep the tongue and mouth moist, staying hydrated, and maintaining a healthy diet.

Body odor. Body odor is due to odor-producing skin bacteria, and it usually smells like vinegar or cheese. Your genes, overall health, and diet can also influence your body odor. Using antiperspirant and deodorant, keeping your body clean and dry, and changing your clothes frequently are the best way to beat body odor.

Funny Smells

Signs that you might be the office odor problem:

1. Coworkers constantly offer you gum, mints, or deodorant.
2. Your coworkers keep air fresheners and potpourri on their desks.
3. Someone gives you soap for your birthday.
4. Every room in the office smells funny when you're in it.

THE #5 *EFFING PROBLEM: BLURRY BUSINESS LINES

Something strange happened in 1956. For the first time in U.S. history, the number of white-collar workers exceeded the number of blue-collar workers. The industrial age was coming to an end and the information age was taking hold. Over the next three decades, computers became more practical and powerful, able to process millions of pieces of data in a matter of seconds. But it was the 1989 birth of the World Wide Web, now known as the Internet, that launched the digital age and forever changed how the world does business.

Thanks to the digital revolution, cell phones, e-mail, social networking websites, and Blackberry

True *Effing Fact

Roughly 247 billion e-mails were sent each day in 2009, according to the technology market research firm the Radicati Group. That's 2.8 million e-mails every second!

devices have blurred the traditional lines between work and play. Today it is hard to determine exactly where work ends and leisure time begins. While personal use of the company Internet is the largest time-wasting activity at work, more than half of all employees check their business e-mail accounts from home at night and on weekends. Surveys suggest that the average American spends more than five hours each week doing work activities on the Internet while off the clock, and nine out of ten employees take work home with them on a regular basis. This hyperconnectivity has made it increasingly difficult to mentally and physically detach ourselves from the office.

Two recent trends exemplify how drastically the work environment has changed. Dalton Conley, a sociologist from New York University, coined the phrase "weisure" to describe the increasing amount of leisure time being spent doing business or quasi-business activities, such as business lunches, dinners, or networking events. Some employees work out at the corporate gym. It has also become routine to tend to some business matters while at dinner with friends or family. Anytime work interfaces with leisure, it's called weisure.

The modern office is undergoing a similar evolution. Some large corporations, most notably the electronics giant Best Buy, have adopted a management style called "ROWE," a results-only work environment. Under the ROWE style of management, employees make their own schedules, and they can choose to work from the office, from home, or even from their favorite coffee shop. There are no meetings, set hours, or time clocks. As long as the work gets done and the results are achieved, there are no questions asked. Proponents of the ROWE revolution say it makes employees happier and boosts productivity; plus, it saves on corporate real estate and other overhead costs.

The evolution of this work-life culture, along with the explosion of social networking websites like Facebook, MySpace, and Twitter, have created brand-new challenges concerning the way we work and the way we live. Our private lives are becoming intertwined with our working lives. Here are some tips on how to avoid some of the most common work-life entanglements.

The *Effing Solution:
Work-Life Balance Workshop

Enjoying your work is a wonderful thing, but being on the job 24–7 can lead to burnout and a steep drop in productivity. Studies suggest that the digital revolution has actually created more leisure time for working Americans, but we are not enjoying it as much as we once did. Occupational stress is at an all-time high, and in our work-life world, it takes effort to escape.

Prioritize pleasure. Life is about enjoyment, not employment. Make sure to do something recreational and fulfilling each day. Being able to enjoy your life is much more important than going to work. Avoid being so deadline driven. While meeting your deadlines at work is extremely important, it should not come at the expense of your private life and emotional health. When setting deadlines, be realistic about the time frame and pace yourself toward that goal.

Simplify your life. Don't overcommit on the job or at home. You can stay out of "juggle jeopardy" by eliminating personal activities that are time-consuming and no longer enjoyable. At work learn how to better delegate or say no to unimportant tasks—of course, do this as diplomatically as possible.

Create a record and a trail. Keep a log of all your work activities, wherever and whenever they occur. This will give you a better idea about how much time you are actually spending on work activities. If there is a stark discrepancy between your pay and the amount of time you are investing, speak to your boss about making some adjustments. Carbon copy (CC) your superiors on all business e-mails that you send from home. If you do research from home, send an e-mail with some thoughts and links to your coworkers or managers. This creates a trail of your off-the-clock work activities and a reminder of your enthusiasm for the project. If you are not going to get paid for your extra efforts, you should at least be acknowledged.

Deliberately disconnect. While most employees would be reluctant to miss or leave work early to tend to a family matter, they rarely hesitate to skip out on family and friends for a work matter. Try to bring more equity into this equation; schedule a regular poker night, a night out with friends, a family night, or a date night. Volunteer for charity work, join a club, or attend religious services. Whatever you choose to do, make it meaningful and make it unbreakable. Turn off your cell phone and close your e-mail. Disconnect completely from your job and reconnect with the important people in your life.

Party smartly. Socializing with your managers and coworkers can put you on the fast track to success or the road to Palookaville. But you can socialize with coworkers and superiors without jeopardizing your career. Watch your alcohol intake carefully at all networking events, happy hours, business lunches, and dinners. Never complain about work or the boss to your coworkers, no matter how close you feel to them. Don't talk about politics or religion with coworkers; it causes much more trouble than it is worth. Instead, get to know your coworkers better by asking about their hobbies, children, families, or aspirations. Never exclude coworkers from large gatherings and parties; it may create long-standing resentments. If you feel like smooching someone you work with, think again. If you are drinking with coworkers, don't take pictures. If you do take pictures, don't post them on your Facebook or MySpace profile.

Imaginary "friends." With the advent of social networking websites, virtual strangers have near complete access to our private lives. On our Facebook and MySpace profiles, these imaginary friends can find out our likes and dislikes, sexual orientation, favorite movies, opinions about mundane topics, and our rambling status updates. Remember: you would not have chosen many of your social networking "friends" as actual friends. People have been fired over updates like, "My job is so boring," and "My boss is clueless." If you have "friended" many coworkers, keep your profile rated PG—don't trash your job or your coworkers, and steer clear of any controversial postings. This is also very important if you are looking for a job. Employers are increasingly using social networking profiles of prospective employees to get a fuller picture of who you are. Adjust your privacy settings. Social networking profiles come with adjustable privacy settings that can limit the content seen by specific people. Use these settings liberally. Set privacy standards in your real life, too. Don't listen to your messages on speaker phone, watch what you say, and don't reveal too much about your personal life while on the job.

THE #6 *EFFING PROBLEM: YOUR BAD BOSS

Employees don't leave their jobs or corporations, they leave their bosses—so the saying goes. According to Working America, a community affiliate of the AFL-CIO, at least one in every ten employees claims to work for a bad boss—that's more than 15 million people. Almost everyone has worked for a dictator or a delegator, a micromanager or a meddler, a slacker or a taskmaster. But being lazy and dishonest are the most common complaints made against bad bosses. In a recent survey, 21 percent of workers said their boss steals credit for their work, and 33 percent said their boss doesn't give them the recognition they deserve. Unfortunately, the struggling economy and tight job market are forcing many workers to stay on the job and under the thumb of a bad boss.

Bad Boss Behavior

Researchers from Florida State University studied more than 700 workers and found:

39 percent said their supervisor did not keep promises.

37 percent said their supervisor failed to give credit when due.

31 percent said their supervisor gave them the "silent treatment".

27 percent said their supervisor made negative comments about them to other employees or managers.

24 percent said their supervisor invaded their privacy.

23 percent said their supervisor blamed others to cover up mistakes or prevent embarrassment.

Having a bad boss may even affect your health. A 2008 study from Sweden found that people who consider their boss unfair, deficient in managerial skills, or inconsiderate are more likely to develop heart disease or suffer a heart attack. The same study found that having a boss who exhibits strong leadership qualities may lower the risk of heart disease. Other studies have shown that having a poor rapport with your boss can increase the risk of depression and other psychological illnesses. In fact, when it comes to causing depression, studies suggest your relationship with your boss may be as important as your relationship with your spouse.

THE *EFFING SOLUTION: BAD BOSS SURVIVAL TIPS

Even terrible bosses may not realize they are being bad bosses. Everyone is capable of being distracted, detached, or over-worked. But for other bosses, the bad behavior is intentional. It's important to know if your boss is acting out of ignorance or out of malice. If your boss is acting out of malice, you may want to involve a human resources (HR) professional early.

It's also important to gauge your coworkers' interactions with your bad boss. Every employee's experience is different. Some work well with tyrannical taskmasters, while others need a more detached management style to thrive. Your bad boss may simply not suit your particular work habits. But every worker has the right to work in a professional environment, and if your work environment is deplorable, you should insist upon correcting the situation. These "Bad Boss Survival Tips" will help you get the best out of your bad boss:

- **Look in the mirror.** If 10 percent of bosses are bad bosses, 90 percent of bosses are good. No doubt there are more bad employees than bad bosses in the workplace, and you might be one of them. Examine your skills and efforts before complaining about or confronting your boss.

- **Watch your work.** Having a bad boss can dramatically impair your work habits. If you are performing poorly, it makes it more difficult to resolve any workplace conflicts. If you have a bad boss, you might feel compelled to call in sick more often, participate in office gossip, complain about your boss, decrease your productivity, or do sloppy work. Make sure you are not making your situation worse. Focus on your work responsibilities and never work against the goals of your boss or your company.

- **Tread carefully.** Unless the issue with your bad boss is egregious, dangerous, or criminal, don't rush to inform superiors or human resources executives. Your boss likely has more corporate support than you do, and you may be portrayed as a troublemaker or a complainer. It is usually best to try to smooth things over with your boss directly, and it may even strengthen your working relationship.

- **Pick the right time.** Be smart in choosing the appropriate time to talk to your boss about improving your relationship. If you plan on an informal meeting, wait for a day when your boss appears to be in a good mood. Later in the week is usually better than earlier in the week. Sometimes making a formal appointment is your best option.

- **Package your problem.** When confronting your bad boss directly, be polite and package the problem as a corporate matter. Don't make it personal. Focus on how the poor work environment is contributing to low performance and how creating a better work environment could lead to improvements in morale and productivity. Always frame your issue as a desire to work better with your boss and the rest of your team.

- **Always keep your cool.** Never react emotionally. Resist urges to shout, scream, use foul language, or cry. If your bad boss is combative or threatening, defer and escape the situation. Take a time-out and collect your thoughts before reapproaching your boss. Emotions cloud judgment.

- **Always keep it private.** Don't complain about your boss to coworkers and don't reveal private conversations or disagreements you have with your boss. If you publicize the issues you are having with your bad boss, it will fuel office gossip, and you will definitely get burned.

- **Always keep a log.** Write down exact dates, times, and circumstances your boss has acted inappropriately. If your boss misbehaves in front of your coworkers, include them in the log as witnesses. If you discuss the problem with your boss, write down the details of the conversation. You may need this log if the human resources department gets involved.

- **Acknowledge positive changes.** If after talking to your bad boss things do improve, make sure you acknowledge the improvement and say "thank you." Never underestimate the power of positive reinforcement.

- **Consider your options.** If your boss does not take measures to improve your relationship, it may be time to speak to the human resources department, seek a transfer within the company, or find another job. Just don't conduct your job search while at work.

- **Keep it all in perspective.** In most cases your boss will not change dramatically. Our work behavior is mostly a reflection of our personalities, and it is very difficult to change someone's personality. Some people are just not meant to work together, and your differences with your bad boss may be irreconcilable. And remember—bad bosses are everywhere. Your current bad boss is not likely your last bad boss. Keep this in mind when you land that new job.

THE #7 *EFFING PROBLEM: TOXIC COWORKERS

You can pick your friends, but under most circumstances you cannot pick your coworkers. Every office has a variety of personalities, and many of them are not pleasant. Having difficulties with other employees can reduce your job satisfaction, decrease your performance, and sabotage your career. Admittedly, coping with corporate bullies, credit-stealers, backstabbers, bimbos, and boneheads can be challenging. Many of your coworkers are not people you would choose to socialize with outside of the office. But you must try your best to work well with each of them.

Ten Toxic Coworkers

Do you recognize yourself or anyone you work with in these profiles?

The Gossip: This nosy neighbor brokers inside information about your coworkers to compensate for their own insecurities.

The Suck-up: This well-positioned butt-kisser parrots the boss's ideas, steals credit from coworkers, and uses flattery to get ahead.

The Complainer: Highly critical of others, this toxic malcontent never has anything positive to say about anybody or anything.

The Borrow Thief: Lend this sticky-handed coworker your stapler at your own risk.

The Know-it-all: This fact-flinger often speaks in jargon or acronyms others do not understand in an attempt to show intellectual dominance.

The Control Freak: This micromanager is an inflexible taskmaster who tries to control projects by controlling people.

The Delegator: Who made this guy or gal the boss? Nobody did, actually.

The Pervert: Ask the female interns; there is at least one creep in every office.

The Sickie: This plague-riddled employee always calls in sick and moans and groans all day about the latest ailment.

The Sicko: Beware of the disgruntled, highly cynical loner.

It is good advice to consider your coworkers like a second family—strange uncles and all. Every member of your office family has a different role and a different way of working. Your job is to recognize your specific role within the family and perform it to the best of your ability. It is also important to recognize the roles of the other family members and assist them in maximizing their contributions. Surveys suggest employees who befriend one another are happier and more productive. But conflicts will inevitably arise in any workplace. You shouldn't expect to have a conflict-free workplace any more than you would expect to have a conflict-free family. Neither one exists. To get ahead in the modern workplace, you will have to play some office politics by making adjustments and accommodations. But you can play politics well and still play nice.

True *Effing Fact

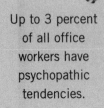

Up to 3 percent of all office workers have psychopathic tendencies.

THE *EFFING SOLUTION: OFFICE HARMONY HELP

All conflicts have a large emotional component, including those that arise between coworkers. Conflicts usually do not arise from purely logical situations, even if the outcome is negative. So addressing the emotions underlying difficulties with coworkers is critical to improving your working relationships or keeping them from falling apart.

Examine why you care. If you are bothered by someone's personality at work, it is important to ask yourself why you are really bothered. You may be jealous of the "office flirt" simply because she is good-looking. You may envy the "workaholic" because he or she is willing to put in the extra time and effort while you are not. The office "know-it-all" might actually know a lot of useful information, and that makes you feel insecure about your own knowledge base. Honestly, analyze your own emotional reaction to the personalities of your coworkers. What makes you dislike them? Many times the problem is not their actions, but your reactions.

Remember their strengths. Your coworkers were hired for a reason. Instead of concentrating on their faults, concentrate on their strengths. Your boss might rely on the encyclopedic knowledge of the office "know-it-all," the office "gossip" might occasionally provide some helpful inside information, and the "control freak" might actually be very productive.

Dig deeper and make allowances. There are many understandable reasons why a person may act strangely at work. Sometimes the odd behavior is situational; perhaps one of your coworkers is going through a divorce or a home foreclosure. Perhaps they were diagnosed with a physical or mental illness. There are plenty of insecurities and events that are manifested as annoying work personalities. Instead of judging and walling off these coworkers, extend a hand to help.

Don't take it personally. Every one of your coworkers will bother you at some point, and you will annoy every one of them in return. Some of your coworkers will dislike your personality from the minute they meet you and never change their opinion. Don't take the dislike personally.

Always act professionally. When involved in a conflict with any difficult coworker, assess the situation and contain your emotions. At times you might feel like exploding, but practicing self-control will preserve your professional image. Do your best to separate your emotions from your reactions. Don't gossip or make fun of the coworker with other employees.

Always be private and discreet. Speak directly to the person you are having the problem with, don't gossip or talk badly about another employee in front of your coworkers. Be tactful in your criticism and solution-oriented in your suggestions. Keep your personal issues discreet and keep all private conversations private.

Spot the troublemakers. Every office has a few hopeless troublemakers and it is best to avoid them as much as possible. They are always fishing for trouble, so don't bite the bait. Resist the urge to befriend office troublemakers; friendship will not spare you their wrath.

Be the office Switzerland. Maintain neutrality in all conflicts between coworkers. Choosing a side could lead to long-standing resentments. Know when to MYOB.

Let it go. Don't hold grudges, and always act to restore workplace harmony. If you have tried and failed to repair a relationship, let it be. If the conflict has been resolved, work to make the relationship stronger.

THE #8 *EFFING PROBLEM: OFFICE GOSSIP

It happens at the water cooler and over hushed cubicle conversations. It happens behind closed doors, in e-mails, and in hallways. It's office gossip, and thanks to the technological revolution, it travels faster and farther than ever before. Lies can be launched and reputations can be ruined with just a few keystrokes and the click of a mouse. Nobody is immune. Every office has a grapevine, and every employee is a gossipy grape from time to time. A 2002 study conducted by Equisys, a business communications company, revealed that the average U.S. employee wastes sixty-five hours each year listening to

True *Effing Fact

Some believe the word "gossip" originated with shifty politicians who would send their assistants to local taverns to "go sip" and eavesdrop on the public. The word actually derives from the Old English "godsibb," a word meaning "godparent." The godparent was present at the childbirth and could spread the news.

or spreading office gossip. A 2007 survey conducted by the staffing firm Randstad USA found that office gossip was the number one pet peeve among American workers.

The tendency to gossip appears to be universal, and studies show that men and women gossip in equal amounts. Roughly 20 percent of all daily conversations could be classified as "gossip," or the peer-to-peer transfer of unproven information. Gossip is such a universal pursuit that many evolutionary psychologists believe it serves several positive functions in society at large: it may foster social bonds between like-minded people, be an efficient means of communicating important personal information between members of a large group, can help large groups establish and enforce behavioral norms, help break social bonds that are no longer supportive, and can be used to enhance power or prestige. One study on workplace gossip found that middle managers get more accurate information about their employees through the office grapevine than they do through more formal channels of communication.

Of course, gossip has a more familiar dark side, and it can erode office morale and decrease productivity. It is most often an attack of malicious innuendo aimed at damaging or destroying another person's reputation, but office gossip can take many other forms. Disgruntled employees may leak corporate strategies to competitors; coworkers may repeat details of a privately held conversation or send a secretive e-mail. Sometimes office gossip is nonverbal, and coworkers may use a sarcastic tone of voice and facial gestures to draw attention to the gossip target.

Low self-esteem, a desire to fit into the corporate social structure, and job insecurity are thought to be the most common motivators for office gossip. Recent research suggests that the problem may be on the increase. A study of human resources executives found that when economic times are tough, complaints about office gossip rise dramatically. But you can protect yourself and help limit the impact of office gossip if you play by the "Rumor Rules."

THE *EFFING SOLUTION: THE RUMOR RULES

Is it kind? Is it true? Is it important?

Most malicious office gossip can be stopped if you ask yourself these three simple questions: Is the information kind and intended to help? Is the information true? Is it important? If you answer "no" to any of these questions, then the information should be killed—no matter how juicy the rumor may seem. If a rumor is unkind but true, kill it. If the rumor is unimportant but true, kill it. And, of course, if you cannot verify the truth of a rumor, kill it. On the other hand, if you learn useful, important, and true information through the office grapevine, feel free to pass it along.

The Rumor Rules

1. Never be the starting point of office gossip. If you spread gossip, your coworkers will learn to never trust you.

2. Never trust the office gossip. If they are spreading rumors about your coworkers, they will spread rumors about you, too.

3. Arm yourself with the facts. There may be a nugget of truth to the rumor, and sometimes that truth may be helpful to your career. If you hear a rumor about a coworker that is concerning to you, speak to them directly.

4. Keep all of your private conversations private. Never violate your confidences.

5. Deflect the gossip. If the office gossiper attempts to relay a rumor to you, say, "I am not comfortable hearing stuff about so-and-so. I wouldn't want people talking about me that way."

6. Disengage the gossiper. Perhaps say, "I have too much work to do."

7. Remember the golden rule: Ask yourself, "Is it kind? Is it true? Is it important?"

If you are the target of office gossip, it is important to examine your behavior. There is usually at least a kernel of truth to most rumors, and if people are talking about your drinking habits at work, you might actually have a drinking problem. If your coworkers portray you as a sex-crazed floozy, you might be dressing or acting inappropriately in the workplace. Analyze and correct any of your behaviors that may be fueling the rumors. If patently false rumors are being spread about you by an individual, a private and polite confrontation is in order. The sooner this is done, the better. Tell the gossiper, "I heard you said _____ _____ about me. It is not true, and it is really hurtful. So please stop. If you have a problem about something I do or say in the office, I would prefer it if you just come talk to me directly next time. I will do my best to clear up any misunderstandings." It is extremely important to keep this conversation private, informal, and as friendly as possible. You should always be working to resolve conflicts, not strain them further—even if you have been insulted. Of course, sometimes rumors will spiral out of control, and some gossips will never keep their mouths shut. If you think office gossip is having an impact on your career and job satisfaction, the issue should be referred to the corporate HR department.

THE #9 *EFFING PROBLEM:
OFFICE ROMANCES

Cupid must have his own cubicle. A 2009 survey of more than eight thousand adults conducted by the online job website Careerbuilder.com found that 10 percent of U.S. employees would like to date someone at their current place of employment, and 40 percent admit to having dated a coworker in the past. Of those, one in five have dated multiple coworkers. Contrary to popular belief, most corporations do not have an official written or verbal policy about on-the-job romances, and the majority of American workers support a romance-friendly workplace. Since we spend considerably more time at work than we do at bars, nightclubs, or visiting online dating sites, looking for love in the office seems like a very logical choice. And for many, that logic pays off. Roughly 20 percent of workers met their spouses at work, and another 10 percent met their spouses through a coworker.

Job "Satisfaction"

Twenty-three percent of U.S. workers claim to have had sex *inside* the workplace. Most often it occurred in the boardroom, bathroom, break room, the boss's office, the cleaning closet, the stairwell, or out in the parking lot.

(Source: Vault.com, Office Romance Survey, 2010)

If you are not careful with your office romance, Cupid's arrow can backfire—big-time. If you are dating a peer, your coworkers may resent your closeness and/or gossip about your relationship, and romantic rivals may react with jealousy. It is also difficult for dating colleagues to separate the working relationship from the romantic relationship. Relationship problems can become a distraction at the office, affecting performance and reducing productivity. In a similar sense, professional rivalries and workplace issues may create romantic difficulties in peer-to-peer relationships.

If you are a manager having a relationship with a subordinate, you are putting your credibility at risk. Often other employees interpret the romantic relationship as favoritism, and your superiors will consider it unprofessional. Relationships between managers and subordinates also raise the risk of sexual harassment allegations. Sexual harassment is a serious offense, and it could cost a corporation millions of dollars.

It is important to keep in mind that all romantic relationships are more likely to fail than succeed—including office romances. So be very careful when dating at work. One messy breakup with the wrong person can ruin your reputation or sabotage your entire career.

THE *EFFING SOLUTION: OFFICE ROMANCE RULES

Office relationships can lead to lifelong love affairs, even if the rules are broken. But most office romances will end like most other romances—in flames. Here are some guidelines that might keep you from getting burned.

Office Romance Rules

1. **Set ground rules.** Discuss with your partner how you plan to keep your professional and personal lives separate. Also discuss what will happen in the event of a breakup.
2. **Keep it quiet.** Don't flaunt your relationship in the office or in front of coworkers. Avoid public displays of affection (PDAs), such as kissing, hugging, or massaging. You do not have to keep your relationship a secret, but you do have to keep it professional.

3. **Keep it honest.** Don't deny your relationship when asked by colleagues or your managers. Being honest about your relationship will help prevent office gossip. Ask your HR representative if the company has a policy against office romances. On rare occasions employees may be asked to sign a relationship contract, also called a "love contract."

4. **Don't date your boss.** It always looks inappropriate, and it is the most dangerous type of office romance. Employees are much more willing to accept a romance between peers than between a coworker and the boss.

5. **No flings with underlings.** If you are the boss, don't date your subordinates; you will lose credibility with the rest of the employees, and it could generate a sexual harassment lawsuit.

6. **No flings with rings.** A 2008 Vault.com survey of employees found nearly half (48 percent) have known a married colleague who was having an affair at work, and 40 percent knew a married colleague who had a tryst while on a business trip. Infidelity is often seen as a serious breach of trust and a major character flaw by other employees.

7. **Never have an affair with the spouse of a colleague.** This is a serious breach of ethics and will only lead to disaster.

8. **The office is off-limits.** The thrill of "doing it" on the desk is not worth a visit to the unemployment office.

9. **Men think twice, women think thrice.** The dating double standard is common in many workplaces; while "boys will be boys," women will be called floozies, bimbos, tramps, or worse.

10. **Don't bring the boardroom into the bedroom, and don't bring the bedroom into the boardroom.**

If you use some common sense, an office romance can blossom into a lifelong love affair. Let's take a look at some famous workplace romances that seem to have worked out all right.

After finishing his first year at Harvard Law School, future president Barack Obama was hired by a prominent Chicago law firm as a summer associate. The firm appointed Michelle Robinson as his advisor. After about one month of working together, Obama finally mustered up enough courage to ask Michelle on a date. She declined. In his autobiography, *The Audacity of Hope*, Obama says he "eventually wore her down."

Actors Humphrey Bogart and Lauren Bacall were legendary for their on-screen and off-screen romantic chemistry. They met while filming the 1944 movie *To Have and Have Not*. It was Bacall's first film; she was nineteen years old. Bogart was forty-five and ending his third marriage. They married and later had two children.

Tom Hanks fell in love with Rita Wilson while filming the movie *Volunteers*. They have been married for more than twenty years. In 1987 Melinda French, a recent MBA graduate, began working at Microsoft, where she eventually became the general manager of information products. That same year she met her future husband, Bill Gates, at a Microsoft press event.

Office romances can blossom—just watch out for the thorns.

THE #10 *EFFING PROBLEM:
THE CORPORATE LADDER MENTALITY

The first rungs on the corporate ladder were probably set in place during the Great Depression when the unemployment rate jumped to nearly 25 percent and half of all Americans were living at or below poverty level. In those dark financial days, a steady paycheck meant personal security for the employee. In turn, employee security meant loyalty for the company. It was a mutually beneficial relationship, and the low job turnover rate following the Great Depression spawned a generation of "company men." Then, following World War II, returning GIs filled up the bottom ranks of U.S. corporations, which added a few more rungs to the ladder. But the GIs also imported the military's hierarchical reward-and-advancement structure to the workplace. This is really when the corporate ladder began to rise and American workers began to climb it.

In today's workplace, climbing the corporate ladder is no longer an effective means of getting ahead. Due to the digital revolution, modern companies must compete in a global marketplace where cheaper competitors are just a few clicks away. To survive, U.S. businesses have had to adapt by becoming more nimble, less dependent on employee reliability, and more dependent on reliable technology. Companies are streamlining, downsizing, and outsourcing like never before. At the same time they are investing fewer resources in the long-term future of their employees, cutting back on benefits like pension plans and health insurance, and hiring part-time or temporary workers.

Many jobs require an advanced degree or special training, and if you don't meet the corporate qualifications, you won't be considered—regardless of your experience in the field or seniority at the company. Today high-priced middle managers and other senior employees are often the first necks stretched across the chopping block. In previous recessions, veteran workers were spared the company ax. With so few businesses rewarding company loyalty, workers are being forced to fend for themselves. Some recent surveys suggest as many as 75 percent of employed workers are currently looking for another job. Frustrated by the lack of company loyalty and career advancement, workers are rebuilding the corporate ladder. They are creating more options for themselves by seeking outside opportunities, taking second jobs, starting their own businesses, or going back to school.

In the modern workplace every employee is a free agent and the CEO of their own career. We are becoming a "freelance economy." Reaching the top requires risk, both upward and lateral moves, position changes, and a little swinging and sliding from place to place. If you want to succeed in business today, you have to step off the corporate ladder and jump onto the corporate jungle gym.

THE *EFFING SOLUTION: HOW TO CLIMB THE CORPORATE JUNGLE GYM

Never stop looking. The modern workplace is fluid and fast-paced, so keep a close eye on your internal and external competitors. Remember, everyone is acting as a free agent, and they are keeping a close eye on you. Many experts even recommend searching for your next job or position as soon as you get hired or promoted. Look for problems to solve, and seek out opportunities. Don't sabotage your success by sitting still. Complacency will kill your career.

Go where the growth is. Many industries are dying, but others are experiencing rapid growth. You must go where the growth is if you want long-term career success. If your current position at the company is becoming less essential, ask for a transfer to a more growth-oriented division. If the entire industry is in decline, abandon ship! Corporate bankruptcies have skyrocketed in recent years, and companies that fail to adapt are routinely forced out of business. Search for jobs in an industry that has a stronger future. In other words, stop trying to sell CDs in an MP3 world. It's also important to live in an area that promises economic opportunity. If the local economy is working against your success, consider moving to a new location.

Hot Jobs of Tomorrow

What are some of the hot jobs of tomorrow? According to the Bureau of Labor Statistics at the U.S. Department of Labor, the occupations below are expected to experience significant growth:

1. Consulting services. Consultants in management, healthcare, and technical and scientific industries
2. Services for the elderly and people with disabilities
3. Gambling industries

4. Home healthcare services
5. Educational services. Roughly one in four Americans are enrolled in an educational institution; somebody has to teach them!
6. Internet publishing and broadcasting

Learn new technologies. You will make yourself less expendable to your current employer and more marketable to future employers by expanding your skill set. Master the latest technologies and incorporate them into your work.

Become an expert. Delve into one particular facet of the corporation and become the go-to employee on all matters relating to it.

Take risks. Seek out challenging assignments. If you succeed you will become the corporate hero. If you fail you will still be learning something very valuable.

Initiate. Generate ideas that may improve productivity or corporate profits.

Lateral is upward. Moving to a lateral position, inside or outside your current company, is a career-boosting move. The change often sparks creative juices and leads to new opportunities. Plus, with each position change, you make more professional contacts.

Use your network. The average job posting today may receive hundreds of applications. The best way to get your résumé noticed is through word of mouth. Working personal connections is extremely important to find a job. If you are looking for a promotion within the company, interact with managers and C-class executives who are not your direct superiors. Build and groom your professional network for jobs outside the corporation.

Find a mentor within the company. Most people who get promotions inside a company have some sort of mentoring relationship with a higher-level employee.

Track your impact. Discover a means of measuring your direct value to your company. It could be sales, net receipts, customers served, hours billed to clients, or the total number of projects completed. Knowing this information will help improve your performance; plus, you can always use the data to impress your boss.

Always "manage up." Manage your boss. Know the likes and dislikes of your direct superior, and learn to anticipate his or her needs. Always make your direct superior look as good as possible. If your manager fails, the entire team looks inept or untrustworthy.

Suicide missions and slides. Sometimes you will be set up to fail by your coworkers or your boss. Recognize these suicide missions, and try to avoid them or plan an escape. It's also important to know when to use the slide on the corporate jungle gym. A tarnished company may tarnish your reputation. In cases of mismanagement, corruption, and criminal activities, it is best to leave the company and slide to safer ground—even if it means taking a lower-level position than your previous employment.

5 The BIG
*Effing Picture

The human brain is composed of more than 100 billion neu-rons. While we all share a basic brain architecture, the brain is exceedingly complex, and no two people are wired in exactly the same way. Even identical twins can have dramatically different personalities, despite sharing the same exact DNA. That's because our life experiences play a prominent role in determining the circuitry of our brains. Major life events, stressful situations, and mental and physical challenges trigger the formation of new connections between neurons. At the same time, existing bonds between brain cells are strengthened, weakened, or dismantled.

To put it another way, your DNA puts the houses in place, but your life experiences pave the roads. This is how human beings learn, and, unfortunately, how we learn to sabotage ourselves. Confronting the underlying negative beliefs of self-sabotage and rewriting dysfunctional psychological scripts is important, but not enough to break the pattern. The real secret to stopping self-sabotage is action. Actions, like those listed in the preceding chapters, help create new experiences, which in turn help rewire the brain for success. Start slowly, because it doesn't happen overnight. It takes time and some reinforcement, but eventually the new connections become the dominant behavioral circuit. And as you are about to read, stopping self-sabotage in one area of life can have a dramatic impact on all others.

HEALTH BENEFITS

Maintaining good health—by quitting smoking, watching your diet, reducing stress, drinking alcohol in moderation, getting adequate sleep and daily exercise—can save your life. But it can also save your romantic relationships—and save you a lot of money. By eating smaller portions at home, you avoid the high calories of restaurant foods, and also their high price. Being at a normal weight reduces the cost of health insurance premiums, raises your job prospects, and may earn you a heftier paycheck.

Studies have shown that thinner workers are more likely to be hired for a job; they get raises more often and are more likely to be promoted within companies when compared to overweight or obese workers. On average, thinner workers earn thousands of dollars more each year. Getting regular exercise has been shown to improve workplace productivity, reduce absences, and lift the burden of work stress. It also improves your love life and your sex life.

Nonsmokers earn significantly more money than smokers, plus they pay a lower cost in health insurance premiums and out-of-pocket healthcare expenses. Nonsmokers are also less likely to get divorced and less likely to experience relationship problems due to sexual dysfunction.

Alcohol abuse or alcoholism is frequently cited as a cause for job loss, divorce, and marital strife, and it takes a devastating toll on children. The booze-binge/hangover combination is one of the most common causes of decreased productivity in the modern workplace.

Getting adequate sleep increases workplace productivity and job satisfaction. Good sleep practices also improve memory and concentration. Reducing stress also makes you happier on the job and at home, plus it helps you get more sleep. So by correcting the *effing problems in your health, you will be improving your finances, career options, and love life.

LOVE CONNECTIONS

Strengthening your romantic relationship will help strengthen your finances and your health. Since the fear of commitment is usually not limited to romantic relationships, overcoming your fear will help you commit to your work, your finances, and your family. Some experts believe the brain chemicals released when falling in love can spark creativity, and having a satisfying sex life has been shown to fuel ingenuity on the job. The same tactics you learned to fight fairly and communicate more effectively with your partner can be used to avoid or defuse tensions in the workplace. Job surveys find that married workers earn more money than singles. Married people also have a higher net worth, and they report more job satisfaction. Several scientific studies have suggested that married people live longer than single or divorced people. Men seem to benefit the most in terms of life span, with married men outliving singles and divorcés by about one year. But women benefit, too. Being happily married in middle age protects against early death, improves overall health, and slows the rate of cognitive decline throughout the senior years for both sexes.

FINANCIAL AID

Money does buy a certain degree of happiness, harmony, and health. Avoiding common financial pitfalls, establishing a household budget, and consistently saving are the surest ways to financial security. Being secure in your finances reduces relationship stress and provides you with more freedom in choosing a career path. Financial security also allows you the ability to indulge your hobbies and fund the dreams of your children.

Identifying sunk costs in your finances will help you identify sunk costs in your professional, personal, and romantic life. Having a little extra money might even add a few extra laughs and a few extra years of life. According to surveys of life satisfaction, people earning the most money are the most likely to report being "very happy." Wealthy people live the longest, while lower-income people have the shortest life span and a much higher burden of chronic diseases, like obesity and type 2 diabetes. And you don't have to be super wealthy to reap the benefits of financial security. Just having a healthy savings account and emergency fund can offset financial duress in the event of a catastrophic illness. Being wealthy will, however, improve your sex life. Studies have shown women have more orgasms with rich men, and wealthy people tend to be more satisfied with their sex lives. Wealthy women report the highest degree of sexual satisfaction.

WORK BONUSES

Eliminating time-wasting activities and overcoming procrastination at work will help you overcome procrastination in other areas of your life, like romance and your health. It will also decrease job stress, decrease the amount of work you take home, and allow you to spend more time by yourself, with friends, or with loved ones. By seeking enjoyment on the job and taking pride in your work, you will start doing the same in your home life. Improving your appearance at work may not only land you a raise, a promotion, and a larger paycheck, if you are a single man, it might also land you a wife.

Improving your job satisfaction will increase your life satisfaction, so finding your dream job just might make all your other dreams come true. Socializing with your coworkers may keep your brain healthier with age. Most people with health insurance receive their benefits through their employer, and a 2009 report from researchers affiliated with Harvard Medical School found lacking health insurance increases the risk of death by 40 percent. Reducing job stress will also help you stay slim, sleep better, alleviate depression, and improve your sex life.

Being compassionate and kind triggers a rush of feel-good brain chemicals called "the helper's high." Kindness also lowers stress, lowers blood pressure, alleviates depression, and boosts the immune system. Recent research suggests it might even help you live longer. Kindness is also contagious, spreading quickly through your social network. So giving to others is often a gift to yourself. Never miss an opportunity to do the right thing. And that brings us to the most important *effing message of this book. In your brilliant new future, always remember to live humbly and love extravagantly.

*Effing Golden Rule

Live humbly;
love extravagantly.

References

CHAPTER 1

The CDC and the National Center for Health Statistics, "Obesity among adults in the United States—No significant change since 2003-2004." *Data Brief* Number 1, November 2007, http://www.cdc.gov/nchs/pressroom/07newsreleases/obesity.htm.

CDC and the National Center for Disease Prevention and Health Promotion, "Healthy youth: childhood obesity," http://www.cdc.gov/HealthyYouth/obesity/.

Barrett L, et al, "pizza power report: PMQ's annual pizza industry analysis." *Pizza Magazine*, 2009, pp. 46–47, http://digital.pmq.com/pizzamagazine/200909/?pg=47.

Sagon C, "Twinkies, 75 years and counting." *The Washington Post*, April 12, 2005, page F01.

The American Dietetic Association, "Ethics opinion: weight loss products and medications." *Journal of the American Dietetic Association* Vol. 108, 2008, pp. 2109–2113.

Teitell B, "The interest in dieting slims down." *The Boston Globe*, September 21, 2008, http://www.boston.com/news/nation/articles/2008/09/21/interest_in_dieting_slims_down/.

Matz J, Frankel E, "The diet survivor's handbook: 60 lessons in eating, acceptance and self-care." (Sourcebooks Inc. 2006) Naperville, IL, http://www.dietsurvivors.com/aboutbook/index.html.

Corsica JA, Pelchat ML, "Food addiction: true or false?" *Current Opinion in Gastroenterology* Vol. 26(2), March 2010, pp. 165–169.

Corwin RL, Grigson PS, "Symposium overview—food addiction: fact or fiction?" *The Journal of Nutrition* Vol. 139(3), January 28, 2009, pp. 617–619.

Cottone P, Sabino V, et al, "Consumatory, anxiety-related and metabolic adaptations in female rats with alternating access to preferred food." *Psychoneuroendocrinology* Vol. 34(1), January 2009, pp. 38–49.

Cottone P, Sabino V, et al, "Opioid-dependent anticipatory negative contrast and binge-like eating in rats with limited access to preferred food." *Neuropsychopharmacolgy* Vol. 33(3), February 2008, pp. 524–525.

Carey DG, et al, "Abdominal fat and insulin resistance in normal and overweight women: direct measurements reveal a strong relationship in subjects at both high and low risk of NIDDM." *Diabetes* Vol. 45, No. 5, May 1996, pp. 633–638.

Pischon T, et al, "General and abdominal adiposity and risk of death in Europe." *New England Journal of Medicine* Vol. 359, November 13, 2008, pp. 2105–2120.

Whitmer RA, et al, "Central obesity and increased risk of dementia more than three decades later." *Neurology*, Vol. 71, March 26, 2008, pp. 1057–1064.

Canoy D, et al, "Body fat distribution and risk of coronary heart disease in men and women in the European Prospective Investigation Into Cancer and Nutrition in Norfolk cohort: a population-based prospective study." *Circulation* 116(25), December 18, 2007, pp. 2933–2943.

The National Weight Control Registry, "Research findings." Accessed February 16, 2010, http://www.nwcr.ws/Research/published%20research.htm.

The National Weight Control Registry, "NWCR facts." Accessed February 16, 2010, http://www.nwcr.ws/Research/default.htm.

Swithers SE, Davidson TL, Martin AA, "High intensity sweeteners and energy balance." *Physiology and Behavior* Epub, Jan 6, 2010.

Swithers SE, et al, "General and persistent effects of high-intensity sweeteners on body weight gain and caloric compensation in rats." *Behavioral Neuroscience* Vol. 123(4), August 2009, pp. 772–780.

Swithers SE, et al, "A role for sweet taste: calorie predictive relations in energy regulation by rats." *Behavioral Neuroscience* Vol. 122(1), February 2008, pp. 161–173.

Davidson T, Swithers S, "A Pavlovian approach to the problem of obesity." *International Journal of Obesity* Vol. 28(7), July 2004, pp. 933–935.

Bellisle F, Drewnowski A, "Intense sweeteners, energy intake and the control of body weight." *European Journal of Clinical Nutrition* Vol. 61(6), June 2007, pp. 691–700.

Wansink B, *Mindless eating: why we eat more than we think*. Bantam Books, 2006, New York, pp. 189–193.

The International Health Racquet and Sportsclub Association (IHRSA), "Profiles of success: The annual industry data survey of the health and fitness club industry—2008." Accessed on February 16, 2010, http://download.ihrsa.org/pubs/profiles-sample.pdf.

Andersen RE, et al, "Effects of lifestyle activity vs. structured aerobic exercise in obese women." *Journal of the American Medical Association* Vol. 281, No. 4, January 27, 1999, pp. 335–340.

Coulson J, et al, "Exercise at work and work performance." *International Journal of Workplace Health Management* Vol. 1,3, 2008, pp. 176–197.

Stenson J, "Exercise may make you a better worker: breaks for physical activity boost job performance, research finds." *MSNBC.com*, July 7, 2005, accessed February 16, 2010, http://www.msnbc.msn.com/id/8160459/ns/health-fitness//.

The Centers for Disease Control, Office of Smoking and Health (OSH), "At a glance 2009: targeting the nation's leading killer." Accessed on February 16, 2010, http://www.cdc.gov/chronicdisease/resources/publications/AAG/osh.htm.

The American Lung Association, "Secondhand smoke fact sheet." Accessed February 16, 2010, http://www.lungusa.org/site/c.dvLUK9O0E/b.35422/.

Helfrich Y, et al, "Effect of smoking on aging of photoprotected skin: Evidence gathered using a new photonumeric scale." *Archives of Dermatology* Vol. 143(3), March 2007, p. 633.

The National Cancer Institute, "Cigarette smoking and cancer: Q and A." Accessed February 16, 2010, http://www.cancer.gov/cancertopics/factsheet/tobacco/cancer.

U.S. Department of Health and Human Services, "The health consequences of involuntary exposure to tobacco smoke: A report of the surgeon general, 2006. Children are hurt by secondhand smoke factsheet." January 4, 2007. Accessed February 16, 2009, http://www.surgeongeneral.gov/library/secondhandsmoke/.

The American Cancer Society, "What are the key statistics for lung cancer?" Accessed February

16, 2010, http://www.cancer.org/docroot/CRI/content/CRI_2_4_1x_What_Are_the_Key_ Statistics_About_Lung_Cancer_15.asp.

Starr J, et al, "Smoking and cognitive change from age 11 to 66 years: a confirmatory investigation." *Addiction Behaviors* Vol. 32, Issue 1, January 2007, pp. 63–68.

Ott A, Andersen K, et al, "Effect of smoking on global cognitive function in nondemented elderly." *Neurology* Vol. 62(6), March 23, 2004, pp. 920–924.

Pasco JA, et al, "Tobacco smoking as a risk factor for major depressive disorder: population based study." *British Journal of Psychiatry* Vol. 193(4), October 2008, pp. 322–326.

Hope BT, et al, "Long term upregulation of protein kinase A and adenylate-cyclase levels in human smokers." *Journal of Neuroscience* Vol. 27(8), February 21 2007, pp. 1964–1972.

Rahman S, Aldoori M, "Smoking and stroke: a causative role." *British Medical Journal* Vol. 317, October 10, 1998, pp. 962–963, http://www.bmj.com/cgi/content/full/317/7164/962.

Wolf PA, et al, "Cigarette smoking as a risk factor for stroke. The Framingham Study." *Journal of the American Medical Association* Vol. 259(7), February 19, 1988.

British Medical Association, "Report on smoking and reproductive health." February 2004. Accessed on February 16, 2010, http://www.bma.org.uk/health_promotion_ethics/tobacco/ smokingreproductivelife.jsp.

Campaign for Tobacco Free Kids, "Tobacco use and impotence." Accessed February 16, 2010, http://www.tobaccofreekids.org/research/factsheets/pdf/0034.pdf.

Illman J, "Health warning! Smoking can seriously shrink your manhood." *Guardian Media Group*, July 26, 1998.

The Centers for Disease Control and Prevention, "Tobacco use and pregnancy." www.cdc.gov, Accessed February 16, 2010, http://www.cdc.gov/reproductivehealth/tobaccoUsePregnancy/ index.htm.

British Medical Association, "Report on Smoking and Reproductive Health." February 2004. Accessed on February 16, 2010, pp 1–10, http://www.bma.org.uk/health_promotion_ethics/ tobacco/smokingreproductivelife.jsp.

U.S Department of Health and Human Services, and the Centers for Disease Control and Prevention. "Preventing smoking and exposure to secondhand smoke before, during and after pregnancy." July 2007.

DiFranza JR, et al, "Symptoms of tobacco dependence after brief intermittent use: the Development and Assessment of Nicotine Dependence in Youth-2 study." *Archives of Pediatrics and Adolescent Medicine* Vol. 161(7), July 2007, pp. 704–710.

Scragg RJ, Difranza JR, et al, "Diminished autonomy over tobacco can appear with the first cigarettes." *Addictive Behaviors* Vol. 33(5) May 2008, pp. 689–698.

DiFranza JR, "Hooked from the first cigarette." *Scientific American* Vol. 298(5), May 2008, pp. 82–87.

Kenfield SA, et al, "Smoking and smoking cessation in relation to mortality in women." *Journal of the American Medical Association* Vol. 299(17), May 2008, pp. 2037–2047.

Gerber Y, et al, "Smoking status and long-term survival after first acute myocardial infarction: a population-based cohort study." *Journal of the American College of Cardiology* Vol. 54(25), December 15, 2009, pp. 2382–2387.

Kinjo K, et al, "Impact of smoking status on long-term mortality in patients with acute myocardial infarction." *Circulation Journal* Vol. 69(1), January 2005, pp. 7–12.

Peterson AV, et al, "Group-randomized trial of a proactive, personalized telephone counseling intervention for adolescent smoking cessation." *Journal of the National Cancer Institute* Vol. 101(20), October 12, 2009, pp. 1378–1392.

Bricker JB, Peterson AV, et al, "Telephone-delivered acceptance and commitment therapy for adult smoking cessation: A feasibility study." *Nicotine and Tobacco Research* Epublication before print, February 8, 2010.

Eisenberg M, Cunningham J, *Canadian Medical Association Journal*, Vol. 179, July 15 2008, News Release, pp.135–146.

Gemenetzidis E, et al, "FOXM1 upregulation is an early event in human squamous cell carcinoma and it is enhanced by nicotine during malignant transformation." *Public Library of Science Online, One* 4(3) e4849, March 16, 2009.

Ingersoll KS, et al, "Combination treatment for nicotine dependence: state of the science." *Substance Use and Misuse* Vol. 40 (13–14), 2005, pp. 1923–1943, 2043–2048.

Dale LC, et al, "Treatment of nicotine dependence." *Mayo Clinic Proceedings* Vol. 75(12), December 2000, pp. 1311–1316.

Tsukahara H, et al, "A randomized controlled open comparative trial of varenicline vs. nicotine patch in adult smokers." *Circulation Journal*, Epub before print February 13, 2010.

Keating GM, et al, "Varenicline: A pharmacoeconomic review of its use as an aid to smoking cessation." *Pharmacoeconomics*, Epub before print, January 27, 2010.

Garrison GD, Dugan SE, "Varenicline: a first-line treatment option for smoking cessation." *Clinical Therapeutics* Vol. 31(3), March 2009, pp. 463–491.

West R, Baker CL, et al, "Effect of varenicline and bupropion SR on craving, nicotine withdrawal symptoms, and rewarding effects of smoking during a quit attempt." *Psychopharmacology* Vol. 197(3), April 2008, pp. 371–377.

Wu TP, et al, "A randomized controlled clinical trial of auricular acupuncture in smoking cessation." *Journal of the Chinese Medical Association* Vol. 70(8), August 2007, pp. 331–338.

Cabioglu MT, et al, "Smoking cessation after acupuncture treatment." *International Journal of Neuroscience* Vol. 117(5), May 2007, pp. 571–578.

White AR, et al, "Acupuncture and related interventions for smoking cessation." *Cochrane Database of Systematic Reviews*, January 25, 2006.

Carmody TP, et al, "Hypnosis for smoking cessation: a randomized trial." *Nicotine and Tobacco Research* Vol. 10(5), May 2008, pp. 811–818.

Elkins G, et al, "Intensive hypnotherapy for smoking cessation: a prospective study." *International Journal of Clinical and Experimental Hypnosis* Vol. 54(3), July 2006, pp. 303–316.

The Centers for Disease Control and Prevention, "Alchohol and Public Health." Accessed on February 16, 2010, http://www.cdc.gov/alcohol/.

The Centers for Disease Control and Prevention, "Trends in mortality from cirrhosis and Alcoholism—United States, 1945–1983." Accessed on February 16, 2010, http://www.cdc.gov/mmwr/preview/mmwrhtml/00000821.htm.

Batty GD, "Childhood mental ability and adult alcohol intake and alcohol problems: the 1970 British cohort study." *American Journal of Public Health* Vol. 98(12), December 2008, pp. 2237–2243.

Di Castelnuovo A, et al, "Prevention of cardiovascular risk by moderate alcohol consumption: epidemiologic evidence and plausible mechanisms." *Internal and Emergency Medicine*, Epub before printing, February 3, 2010.

Grønbaek M, "Epidemiologic evidence for the cardioprotective effects associated with consumption of alcoholic beverages." *Pathophysiology* Vol. 10(2), April 2004, pp. 83–92.

Rubio G, et al, "Efficacy of physician-delivered brief counseling intervention for binge drinkers." The American Journal of Medicine Vol. 123(1), January 2010, pp. 72–78.

The National Institute on Alcohol Abuse and Alcoholism, "Naltrexone or specialized alcohol counseling an effective treatment for alcohol dependence when delivered with medical management." May 2, 2006. Accessed February 16, 2010, http://www.niaaa.nih.gov/News Events/NewsReleases/COMBINERelease.htm.

O'Farrell TJ, et al, "Behavioral family counseling for substance abuse: A treatment development pilot study." *Addictive Behaviors* Vol. 35(1), January 2010, pp. 1–6.

Longabaugh R, Morgenstern J, "Cognitive-behavioral coping-skills therapy for alcohol dependence: current status and future directions." *Alcohol Research and Health.* Vol. 23(2), 1999, pp. 78–85.

Sellman J, et al, "A randomized controlled trial of motivational enhancement therapy (MET) for mild to moderate alcohol dependence." *Journal of Studies on Alcohol* Vol. 62(3), May 2001, pp. 389–396.

Lachance H, et al, "What makes group MET work? A randomized controlled trial of college student drinkers in mandated alcohol diversion." *Psychology of Addictive Behaviors* Vol. 23(4), December 2009, pp. 598–612.

The Centers for Disease Control and Prevention, "National overview of sexually transmitted diseases (STD) 2008." Accessed February 16, 2010, http://www.cdc.gov/std/stats08/natover view.htm.

The Centers for Disease Control and Prevention, "HIV/AIDS in the United States." Revised August, 2009. Accessed February 16, 2010, http://www.cdc.gov/hiv/resources/factsheets/ us.htm.

The Centers for Disease Control, "Healthy youth: sexual risk behaviors." October 23, 2008. Accessed February 16, 2010, http://www.cdc.gov/HealthyYouth/sexualbehaviors/.

Sharples T, "More midlife (and older) STDs." *Time Magazine* July 2, 2008. Accessed February 16, 2010, http://www.time.com/time/health/article/0,8599,1819633,00.html.

Kotz D, "Sex ed for seniors: you still need those condoms." *US News and World Report*, August 5, 2007. Accessed February 16, 2010, http://health.usnews.com/usnews/health/articles/ 070805/13senior.htm.

The National Women's Health Information Center, U.S. Department of Health and Human Services, "Chlamydia: frequently asked questions." Accessed February 16, 2010, http:// www.womenshealth.gov/faq/chlamydia.cfm.

Centers for Disease Control and Prevention, http://www.cdc.gov.

D'Souza G, et al, "Case control study of human papillomavirus and oropharyngeal cancer." *New England Journal of Medicine* Vol. 356(19), May 10, 2007, pp. 1944–1956.

The Guttmacher Institute, "The Guttmacher policy report: family planning clinics prevent 1.4 million unplanned pregnancies annually, save billions of government dollars." *Guttmacher Policy Review* Vol. 11, Number 3, Summer 2008.

Lyles CM, et al, "Best-evidence interventions: findings from a systematic review of HIV behavioral interventions for US populations at high risk, 2000–2004." *American Journal of Public Health.* Vol. 91(1), January 2007, pp. 133–143.

Oriel JD, et al, "Identification of people at high risk of genital HPV infections." *Scandinavian Journal of Infectious Disease* Vol. 69, 1990, pp. 169.

Langer G, Arnedt C, and Sussman D, "Poll: American sex survey, a peak beneath the sheets." October 21, 2004. Accessed on February 16, 2010, http://abcnews.go.com/Primetime/ PollVault/story?id=156921&page=1.

Fryar CD, et al, "Drug use and sexual behaviors reported by adults: United States, 1999–2002." *National Health and Nutrition Examination Survey*, June 28, 2007, the Centers for Disease Control and Prevention. Accessed February 16, 2010, http://www.cdc.gov/nchs/data/ad/ ad384.pdf.

Kolata G, "Sex surveys don't add up." *The New York Times*, August 12, 2007.

Centers for Disease Control and Prevention, "Condoms and STDs: Fact sheet for public health personnel." Accessed February 16, 2010, http://www.cdc.gov/condomeffectiveness/latex.htm.

Winer R, et al, "Condom use and the risk of genital human papillomavirus infection in young women." *New England Journal of Medicine* Vol. 354, Number 25, June 22, 2006, pp. 2645–2654.

National Sleep Foundation, "2009 sleep in america poll," *The National Sleep Foundation*, March 2, 2009.

Goleman D, "Feeling sleepy? The urge to nap is built in." *New York Times*, September 12, 1989. Accessed February 16, 2010, http://www.nytimes.com/1989/09/12/science/feeling-sleepy-an-urge-to-nap-is-built-in.html?pagewanted=1.

Van Der Werf YD, et al, "Learning by observation requires an early sleep window." *Proceedings of the National Academy of Sciences* Vol. 106(45), November 10, 2009, 18926–18930.

Tucker MA, "The impact of sleep duration and subject intelligence on declarative and motor memory performance: how much is enough?" *Journal of Sleep Research* Vol. 18(3), September 2009, pp. 304–312.

Marshall L, et al, "The contribution of sleep to hippocampus-dependent memory consolidation." *Trends in Cognitive Science* Vol. 11(10),October 2007, pp. 442–450.

Born J, et al, "Sleep to remember." *Neuroscientists.* Vol. 12(5), October 2006, pp. 410–424.

Datta S, et al, "Avoidance task training potentiates phasic pontine-wave density in the rat: A mechanisms for sleep-dependent plasticity." *The Journal of Neuroscience* Vol. 20(22), November 15, 2000, pp. 8607–8613.

Kudrimoti HS, et al, "Reactivation of hippocampal cell assemblies: Effects of behavioral state, experience, and EEG dynamics." *The Journal of Neuroscience* Vol. 19(10), May 15, 1999, pp. 4090–4101.

Gorman C, "Why we sleep." *Time Magazine*, December 17, 2004. Accessed on February 16, 2010, http://www.time.com/time/magazine/article/0,9171,1009765-1,00.html.

Zoler ML, "Sleep deprivation may trigger insulin resistance." *Clinical Psychiatry News* Vol. 29(10), October 2001, pp. 27.

Reuters, "Too little sleep tied to increased cancer risk." November 17, 2008. Accessed February 16, 2010, http://www.reuters.com/article/idUSTRE4AG7B520081117.

American Academy of Sleep Medicine, "Regular daily exercise does not increase total sleep time." *Science Daily*, June 8. 2009. Accessed February 16, 2010, http://www.sciencedaily.com/releases/2009/06/090608071937.htm.

Helgesson O, et al, "Self-reported stress levels predict subsequent breast cancer in a cohort of Swedish women." *European Journal of Cancer Prevention* Vol. 12(5), October 2003, 377–381.

Sephton SE, et al, "Depression, cortisol, and suppressed cell-mediated immunity in metastatic breast cancer." *Brain, Behavior and Immunity* Vol. 23(8), November 2009, pp. 1148–1155.

Gidron Y, et al, "Psychosocial factors, biological mediators, and cancer prognosis: a new look at an old story." *Current Opinion in Oncology* Vol. 20(4), July 2008, pp. 386–392.

Wittstein IS, Thiemann DR, et al., "Neurohumoral features of myocardial stunning due to sudden emotional stress." *The New England Journal of Medicine* Vol. 352(6), February 10, 2005, pp. 539–548.

Levitin DJ, Tirovolas AK, "Current advances in the cognitive neuroscience of music." *Annals of the New York Academy of Sciences* Vol. 1156, March 2009, pp. 211–231.

Levitin DJ, "Sing brain, sing." *Newsweek* Vol. 152(12), September 22, 2008, p. 58.

Koelsch S, "Investigating emotion with music: neuroscientific approaches." *Annals of the New York Academy of Sciences* Vol. 1060, December 2005, pp. 412–418.

Koelsch S, et al, "Investigating emotion with music: an fMRI study." *Human Brain Mapping* Vol. 27(3), March 2006, pp. 239–250.

Koyama M, et al, "Recreational music-making modulates immunological responses and mood states in older adults." *Journal of Medical and Dental Sciences* Vol. 56(2), June 2009, pp. 79–90.

Bradt J, Dileo C, "Music for stress and anxiety reduction in coronary heart disease patients." *Cochrane Database of Systematic Reviews* Vol. 15(2), April 15, 2009. Online publication.

Nilsson U, "The anxiety- and pain-reducing effects of music interventions: a systematic review." *AORN Journal* Vol. 87(4), April 2008, pp. 780–807.

Becknell ME, et al, "Effects of listening to heavy metal music on college women." *College Student Journal* Vol. 42(1), March 1, 2008, pp. 24–35.

Kemper K, et al, "Music as therapy." *Southern Medical Journal* Vol. 98(3), March 1, 2005, pp. 282–288.

Setzer WN, "Essential oils and anxiolytic aromatherapy." *Natural Product Communications* Vol. 4(9), September 2009, pp. 1305–1316.

Perry N, Perry E, "Aromatherapy in the management of psychiatric disorders: clinical and neuropharmacological perspectives." *CNS Drugs* Vol. 20(4), 2006, pp. 257–280.

Butje A, et al, "Healing scents: an overview of clinical aromatherapy for emotional distress." *Journal of Psychosocial Nursing and Mental Health Services* Vol. 46(10), October 2008, pp. 46–52.

Martin RA, "Humor, laughter, and physical health: methodological issues and research findings." *Psychological Bulletin* Vol. 127(4), July 2001, pp. 504–519.

Hassed C, "How humor keeps you well." *Australian Family Physician* Vol. 30(1), January 2001, pp. 25–28.

Strean WB, "Laughter prescription." *Canadian Family Physician* Vol. 55(10), October 2009, pp. 965–967.

Nidich SI, et al, "A randomized controlled trial on effects of the Transcendental Meditation program on blood pressure, psychological distress, and coping in young adults." *American Journal of Hypertension* Vol. 22(12), December 2009, pp. 1326–1331.

University of Oregon, "Body-mind meditation boosts performance, reduces stress." *ScienceDaily*, October 9, 2007. Accessed February 17, 2010, http://www.sciencedaily.com/releases/2007/10/071008193437.htm.

Chiesa A, et al, "A systematic review of neurobiological and clinical features of mindfulness meditations." *Psychological Medicine*, November 27, 2009, pp. 1–14.

American Society of Microbiology, "People's hand-washing tales a whitewash, study says." September 18, 2000. Accessed on February 17, 2010, http://archives.cnn.com/2000/HEALTH/09/18/hand.washing/.

CleanphIRST.com, "You wash your hands, but does everyone else?" September 21, 2009. Accessed February 17, 2010, http://www.cleanphirst.com/cleaning-information-news/2009/09/you-wash-your-hands-but-does-everyone.html.

Minnesota Department of Health, "Handwashing: prevent disease and outbreak intervention." 2005. Accessed on February 17, 2010, http://www.health.state.mn.us/handhygiene/curricula/curriculumadult.pdf.

University of Colorado, "CU-Boulder map of human bacterial diversity shows wide interpersonal differences," November 5, 2009. Accessed on February 17, 2010, http://www.colorado.edu/news/r/22ff22190dc1fb08aaae7396565bb0ca.html.

University of Colorado, "Women have more diverse hand bacteria than men, according to CU-Boulder Study." November 3, 2008. Accessed on February 17, 2010, http://www.colorado.edu/news/r/e13276bf11f17a902f6e68a7c364a13b.html.

Centers for Disease Control and Prevention, "Wash your hands." April 27, 2009. Accessed on February 17, 2010, http://www.cdc.gov/Features/HandWashing/.

Centers for Disease Control and Prevention, "Clean hands save lives." November 19, 2009, Accessed on February 17, 2010, http://www.cdc.gov/cleanhands/.

Rabie T, Curtis V, "Handwashing and the risk of respiratory infections: a quantitative systematic review." *Tropical Medicine and International Health* Vol. 11, Number 3, March 2006, pp. 258–267.

Society for General Microbiology, "Handwashing more important than isolation in controlling MRSA superbug infection, study suggests." *Science Daily*, March 31, 2009. Accessed on February 17, 2010, http://www.sciencedaily.com/releases/2009/03/090330200708.htm.

Tork USA, "Dry hands are 1000 times safer than damp hands: washing hands properly becomes increasingly important during the flu season." September 10, 2009. Accessed February 17, 2010, http://www.torkusa.com/Pages/News/News.aspx?id=177685.

Patrick DR, Findon G, et al, "Residual moisture determines the level of touch-contact-associated bacterial transfer following hand washing." *Epidemiology and Infection* Vol. 119(3), December 1997, pp. 319–325.

Prayson B, et al, "Fast food hamburgers: What are we really eating?" *Annals of Diagnostic Pathology* Vol. 12(6), December 2008, pp. 406–409. Accessed on February 17, 2010, http://www.tissuepathology.typepad.com/files/prayson_anndiagpath_dec2008.pdf.

Wansink B, *Mindless eating: why we eat more than we think*. Bantam Books, 2006, New York, pp. 70–75, 182–183.

Sprangler R, et al, "Opiate-like effects of sugar on gene expression in reward areas of the rat brain." *Brain Research* Vol. 124(2), May 19, 2004, pp. 134–142.

Society for the Study of Ingestive Behavior, "High fat, high sugar foods alters brain receptors." July 28, 2009. Accessed February 17, 2010, http://www.ssib.org/web/index.php?page=press&release=2009-1.

Sanders L, "Junk food turns rats into addicts: bacon, cheesecake and Ho-Hos alter pleasure centers in rats' brains." *Science News* Vol. 167(11), November 21, 2009, pp. 8.

Hellmich N, "Soda drinkers consume more calories." *USA Today*, March 26, 2007. Accessed February 17, 2010, http://www.usatoday.com/news/health/2007-03-25-sodadrinkers_N.htm.

The Institute of Medicine, "To err is human: building a safer health system." *The National Academy of Sciences*, November 1, 1999.

Leape LL, et al, "A conversation on medical injury." *Public Health Reports* Vol. 114(4), July-August 1999, pp. 302–317.

Leape LL, et al, "Five years after to err is human: what have we learned?" *The Journal of the American Medical Association* Vol. 293(19), May 18, 2005, pp. 2384–2390.

Centers for Disease Control and Prevention, "Fast Stats." Used for statistics on deaths due to motor vehicle accidents, breast cancer, and HIV/AIDS. Accessed February 17, 2010, http://www.cdc.gov/nchs/FASTATS/acc-inj.htm.

Szabo L, "Number of Americans taking antidepressants doubles." *USA Today*, August 4, 2009. Accessed on February 17, 2010, http://www.usatoday.com/news/health/2009-08-03-antidepressants_N.htm.

Olfson M, Marcus SC, "National patterns in antidepressant medication treatment." *Archives of General Psychiatry* Vol. 66(8), August 2009, 848–856.

Hartz AJ, et al, "Hospital characteristics and mortality rates." *New England Journal of Medicine* Vol. 321(5), December 21, 1989, pp. 1720–1725.

Birkmeyer JD, et al, "Hospital volume and surgical mortality in the United States." *New England Journal of Medicine* Vol. 346(15), April 11, 2002, pp. 1128–1127.

Kostis WJ, et al, "Weekend versus weekday admission and mortality from myocardial infarction." *New England Journal of Medicine* Vol. 356(11), March 15, 2007, pp. 1099–1109.

Bell CM, et al, "Mortality among patients admitted to hospitals on weekends as compared with weekdays." *New England Journal of Medicine* Vol. 345(9), August 30, 2001, pp. 663–668.

CHAPTER 2

Darn Divorce, "Divorce rates around the world." April 8, 2007. Accessed February 17, 2010. http://www.darndivorce.com/divorce-rates-around-the-world/.

Divorce Magazine, "The percentage of new marriages that will end in divorce, in selected countries (2002)." Accessed February 17, 2010, http://www.divorcemag.com/statistics/stats World.shtml.

Walum H, et al, "Genetic variation in the vasopressin receptor 1a gene (AVPR1A) associates with pair-bonding behavior in humans." *Proceedings of the National Academy of Sciences* Vol. 105(37), September 16, 2008, pp. 14153–14156.

Macrae F, "Women talk three times as much as men, says study." *Mail Online*, November 28, 2006. Accessed on February 17, 2010, http://www.dailymail.co.uk/femail/article-419040/Women-talk-times-men-says-study.html.

Mehl MR, et al, "Are women really more talkative than men?" *Science* Vol. 317(5834), July 6, 2007, pp. 82.

Mehrabian A, et al, "Decoding of inconsistent communications." *Journal of Personality and Social Psychology* Vol. 6(1), 1967, pp. 109–114.

Mehrabian A, et al, "Inference of attitudes from nonverbal communication in two channels." *Journal of Consulting Psychology* Vol. 31(3), 1967, pp. 248–252.

Harburg E, et al, "Marital pair anger-coping types may act as an entity to affect mortality: preliminary findings from a prospective study (Tecumseh, Michigan, 1971–1988)." *Journal of Family Communication* Vol. 8(1), 2008, pp. 44–61.

LiveScience, "Spouses who fight live longer." *LiveScience.com*, January 23, 2008. Accessed February 17, 2010, http://www.livescience.com/health/080123-spouse-fights.html.

Eaker E, et al, "Marital status, marital strain, and risk of coronary heart disease or total mortality: the framingham offspring study." *Psychosomatic Medicine* Vol. 69, July 18, 2007, pp. 509–513.

Davies PT, et al, "Adrenocortical underpinnings of children's psychological reactivity to interparental conflict." *Child Development* Vol. 79(6), November-December 2008, pp. 1693–1706.

Sotgui I, Mormont C, "Similarities and differences between traumatic and emotional memories: review and directions for future research." *The Journal of Psychology* Vol. 142(5), September 2008, 449–469.

Elmer-Dewitt P, et al, "Behavior: now for the truth about Americans and sex." *Time Magazine*, October 17, 1994. Accessed on February 17, 2010, http://www.time.com/time/magazine/article/0,9171,981624-1,00.html.

Wellings K, et al, "Sexual behavior in context." *The Lancet* Vol. 368(9548), November 11, 2006, pp. 1706–1728.

Smith T, "American sexual behavior: trends, socio-demographic differences, and risk behavior." The National Opinion Research Center, University of Chicago, December 1998. Accessed February 17, 2010, http://cloud9.norc.uchicago.edu/dlib/t-25.htm.

Sine R, "Sex drive: How do men and women compare?" *WebMD*. Accessed February 17, 2010, http://www.webmd.com/sex/features/sex-drive-how-do-men-women-compare.

Doherty K, "10 surprising health benefits of sex." Accessed February 17, 2010, http://www.webmd.com/sex-relationships/features/10-surprising-health-benefits-of-sex.

Ebron A, "The state of our unions: women reveal what they really think about their marriages." *Women's Day* and *AOL Living*. Accessed February 17, 2010, http://living.aol.com/marriage-poll-results.

Weaver J, "Love, lust and loyalty: many cheat for a thrill, more stay true for love." MSNBC.com/iVillage, April 16, 2007. Accessed February 17, 2010, http://www.msnbc.msn.com/id/17951664/.

Parker-Pope T, "Love, sex, and the changing landscape of infidelity." *The New York Times*, October 27, 2008.

Treas J, Gieden D, "Sexual infidelity among married and cohabiting Americans." *Journal of Marriage and the Family* Vol. 62(1), 2000, pp. 48–60.

The Kinsey Institute, "Frequently asked sexuality questions to the Kinsey Institute." www.kinseyinstitute.org, February 29, 2008. Accessed February 17, 2010, http://www.kinseyinstitute.org/resources/FAQ.html#Treas.

Saltz G, "Do men cheat for the thrill, or the sex?" *Today* at MSNBC.com, May 15, 2007. Accessed February 17, 2010, http://today.msnbc.msn.com/id/18096687/.

Weiss P, "The affairs of men." *New York Magazine*, May 18, 2008. Accessed February 17, 2010, http://nymag.com/relationships/sex/47055/.

Lerche Davis J, "Cheating wives: women and infidelity." *WebMD*. Accessed February 17, 2010, http://www.webmd.com/sex-relationships/features/cheating-wives.

Scheidel W, "Monogamy and polygyny in Greece, Rome, and world history." *Princeton/Stanford Working Papers in Classics* June 2008. Accessed February 17, 2010, http://www.princeton.edu/~pswpc/pdfs/scheidel/060807.pdf.

New World Encyclopedia, "Polygyny." Accessed February 17, 2010, http://www.newworldencyclopedia.org/entry/Polygyny.

Barash DP, Lipton JE, *The myth of monogamy: fidelity and infidelity in animals and people.* Henry Holt, New York, 2001, pp. 11–17.

Barash DP, "Deflating the myth of monogamy." Trinity.edu, Trinity University. Accessed February 17, 2010, http://www.trinity.edu/rnadeau/fys/barash%20on%20monogamy.htm.

Science Daily, "The secret sex lives of swans under scrutiny in new study." June 8, 2006, Accessed February 17, 2010, http://www.sciencedaily.com/releases/2006/06/060607170545.htm.

ABC News, "Infidelity: is monogamy just a myth?" ABC.com. Accessed February 17, 2010, http://abcnews.go.com/2020/Stossel/story?id=5380175&page=2.

Shea C, "Who's your daddy? could 10 percent of men really be deceived about the paternity of the children they're raising? Evolutionary psychologists want to know." *The Boston Globe*, August 20, 2006, Accessed on February 17, 2010, http://www.boston.com/news/globe/ideas/articles/2006/08/20/whos_your_daddy/.

Anderson K, "How well does paternity confidence match actual paternity? Evidence from worldwide nonpaternity rates." *Current Anthropology* Vol. 47(3), June 2006, pp. 513–520.

Bellis M, et al, "Measuring paternal discrepancy and its public health consequences." *Journal of Epidemiology and Community Health* Vol. 59, June 22, 2005, pp. 749–754.

Lucassen A, Parker M, "Revealing false paternity: Some ethical considerations." *The Lancet* Vol. 357(9261), March 2001, pp. 1033–1035.

Sussman LN, "Blood grouping tests in undisputed paternity proceedings." *Journal of the American Medical Association* Vol. 164(3), 1957, pp. 249–250.

American Association of Blood Banks, *Annual Report 2006.*

Panke ES, et al, "Parentage testing using DNA." Accessed February 18, 2010. http://www.utdol.com/patients/content/topic.do?topicKey=~FtfHYEk4cpy4pcM.

Amato P, et al, "People's reasons for divorcing: gender, social class, the life course, and adjustment." *Journal of Family Issues* Vol. 24(5), July 2003, pp. 602–626.

MSNBC.com/iVillage, "Your unadulterated thoughts on adultery." *The Love, Lust and Loyalty Survey*, April 16, 2007.

Hicks T, Leitenberg H, "Sexual fantasies about one's partner versus someone else: gender differences in incidence and frequency." *The Journal of Sex Research* Vol. 38(1), February 2001, pp. 43–50.

Fisher H, Aron A, Brown L, "Romantic love: An fMRI study of a neural mechanism for mate choice." *The Journal of Comparative Neurology* Vol. 493 (1), December 5, 2005, pp. 58–62.

Aron A, Fisher H, et al, "Reward, motivation, and emotion systems associated with early-stage intense romantic love." *Journal of Neurophysiology* Vol. 94(1), July 2005, 327–337.

Fisher H, et al, "Defining the brain systems of lust, romantic attraction, and attachment." *Archives of Sexual Behavior* Vol. 31(5), October 2001, pp. 413–419.

Kluger J, "The science of romance: why we love." *Time Magazine*, January 17, 2008. Accessed on Feburary 18, 2010, http://www.time.com/time/magazine/article/0,9171,1704672,00.html.

Fahmy M, "In love? It's not enough to keep a marriage, study finds." *Reuters.com*, July 14, 2009. Accessed February 18, 2010, http://www.reuters.com/article/idUSSP483675.

Science Daily, "Ugly truth about one night stands: men less choosy than women." *Science Daily.com*, August 12, 2009. Accessed February 18, 2010, http://www.sciencedaily.com/releases/2009/08/090811080749.htm.

Campbell A, "The morning after the night before: affective reactions to one night stands among mated and unmated women and men." *Human Nature* Vol. 19(2), June 2008, pp. 157–173.

Conner S, "Men like casual sex more than women—scientific fact." *The Independent*, June 26, 2008. Accessed February 18, 2010, http://www.independent.co.uk/news/science/men-like-casual-sex-more-than-women-ndash-scientific-fact-854323.html.

ArticleBase.com, "1000 women have their say in a recent survey." March 17, 2009. Accessed February 18, 2010, http://www.articlesbase.com/womens-issues-articles/1000-women-have-their-say-in-a-recent-survey-819559.html.

Risher B, "Pick up lines that work." *Men's Health Magazine.* Accessed February 18, 2010, http://www.menshealth.com/men/sex-relationships/hooking-up/dating-tips-the-art-of-the-pickup-line/article/214924072f8a4110VgnVCM20000012281eac.

Weir W, "Dumb pick up lines are revealing, study says." *The Seattle Times*, September 3, 2007. Accessed February 18, 2010, http://seattletimes.nwsource.com/html/nationworld/2003866249_pickup03.html.

Greengross G, et al, "Dissing oneself versus dissing rivals: effects of status, personality, and sex on the short-term and long-term attractiveness of self-deprecating and other-deprecating humor." *Evolutionary Psychology* Vol. 6(3), 2008, pp. 393–408.

Science Daily, "What men and women say and do in choosing romantic partners are two different matters." *ScienceDaily.com,* February 14, 2008, Accessed February 18, 2010. http://www.science daily.com/releases/2008/02/080213133337.htm.

Springen K, "The real laws of attraction." *Newsweek,* February 14, 2008. Accessed February 18, 2010, http://www.newsweek.com/id/111024.

Hough A, "Men 'prefer curvy women to those who are a size zero', study claims." *Telegraph.co.uk,* October 28, 2009. Accessed February 18, 2010, http://www.telegraph.co.uk/science/science-news/6449941/Men-prefer-curvy-women-to-those-those-who-are-size-zero-study-claims.html.

Singh SM, Singh D, "Optimal waist-to-hip ratios in women activate neural rewards centers in men." *Public Library of Science* Vol. 5(2), February 5, 2010, e9042.

Fisher ML, Voracek M, "The shape of beauty: determinants of female physical attractiveness." *Journal of Cosmetic Dermatology* Vol. 5(2), June 2006, pp. 190–194.

Buss DM, Shackelford TK, "Attractive women want it all: Good genes, economic investment, parenting proclivities, and emotional commitment." *Evolutionary Psychology* Vol. 6(1), May 2008, pp. 134–146.

Black R, "Secrets of attraction may lie in immune system DNA that's sensed through sweat." *The NY Daily News,* February 17, 2010.

Milinski M, "The major histocompatibility complex, sexual selection, and mate choice." *Annual Review of Ecology, Evolution and Systematics* Vol. 37, July 27, 2006, pp. 159–186.

Westneat DF, et al, "Alternative hypotheses linking the immune system and mate choice for good genes." *Proceedings of the Royal Society: Biological Sciences* Vol. 265(1401), June 22, 1998, pp. 1065–1073.

Varian HR, "Online dating? Thin and rich works here too." *New York Times,* June 30, 2005.

Hitsch GJ, et al, "What makes you click: An empirical analysis of online dating." 2006, Working Paper. Accessed February 18, 2010, http://www.aeaweb.org/annual_mtg_papers/2006/0106 _0800_0502.pdf.

Leake J, "Wealthy men give women more orgasms." *Times Online,* January 18, 2009. Accessed February 18, 2010, http://www.timesonline.co.uk/tol/news/science/article5537017.ece.

CHAPTER 3

Leonhardt D, "Maybe money does buy happiness after all." *The New York Times,* April 16, 2008.

Begley S, "Why money doesn't buy happiness." *Newsweek,* October 15, 2007. Accessed February 18, 2010, http://www.newsweek.com/id/43884.

Bennett D, "Happiness: A buyer's guide." *The Boston Globe,* August 23, 2009. Accessed February 18, 2010, http://www.boston.com/bostonglobe/ideas/articles/2009/08/23/happiness_a_buyers_guide/.

Easterlin R, "Income and happiness: towards a unified theory." *The Economic Journal* Vol. 111, July 2001, pp. 465–484.

Brooks AC, "Can money buy happiness?" *The American,* May-June 2008. Accessed February 18, 2010, http://www.american.com/archive/2008/may-june-magazine-contents/can-money-buy-happiness.

Leake J, "Wealthy men give women more orgasms." *Times Online,* January 18, 2009. Accessed February 18, 2010, http://www.timesonline.co.uk/tol/news/science/article5537017.ece.

Herper M, "Now it's a fact: money doesn't buy happiness." *Forbes Magazine,* September 23, 2004. Accessed February 18, 2010, http://moneycentral.msn.com/content/invest/forbes/ P95294.asp.

Brickman P, et al, "Lottery winners and accident victims: is happiness relative?" *Journal of Personality and Social Psychology* Vol. 36(8), August 1978, 917–927.

Grinnell R, "Money = happiness, but there's a catch." *PsychCentral.com*. Accessed February 18, 2010, http://psychcentral.com/blog/archives/2009/02/08/money-happiness-but-theres-a-catch/.

Landau E, "Study: experiences make us happier than possessions." *CNN.com* February 10, 2009. Accessed February 18, 2010. http://www.cnn.com/2009/HEALTH/02/10/happiness.possessions/index.html.

Forbes, "Why billionaires live longer." April 6, 2005. Accessed February 18, 2010 http://moneycentral.msn.com/content/invest/forbes/P114177.asp.

Bosma H, et al, "Socioeconomic inequalities in mortality and importance of perceived control." *British Medical Journal* Vol. 319, December 4, 1999, pp. 1469–1470.

Khan K, "How does your debt compare?" *MSN Money*. Accessed February 18, 2010, http://moneycentral.msn.com/content/SavingandDebt/P70581.asp.

Crutsinger M, "Few pennies saved: Americans spending more than they earn." *Associated Press*, February 2, 2007.

Herbert B, "Recession? What recession?" *The New York Times*, Opinion, November 10, 2007.

Holland LH, and Ewalt DM, "How Americans make and spend their money." *Forbes.com*, July 17, 2006. Accessed February 18, 2010, http://www.forbes.com/2006/07/19/spending-income-level_cx_lh_de_0719spending.html.

Bureau of Economic Analysis, Personal Savings Rate. Accessed February 18, 2010, http://www.bea.gov/BRIEFRM/SAVING.HTM.

Associated Press, "U.S. savings rate hits lowest level since 1933." *MSNBC.com*, January 30, 2006. Accessed February 18, 2010 http://www.msnbc.msn.com/id/11098797/.

The Employee Benefit Research Institute, "The 2009 retirement confidence survey: economy drives confidence to record lows; many looking to work longer." *EBRI Issue Brief #328*, April 2009. Accessed February 18, 2010, http://www.ebri.org/publications/ib/index.cfm?fa=ibdisp&content_id=4226.

Francis DR, "Economic scene: U.S. begins crackdown on CEO pay. Will it work?" *Christian Science Monitor*, September 10, 2009. Accessed February 18, 2010, http://www.csmonitor.com/Money/2009/0910/economic-scene-us-begins-crackdown-on-ceo-pay-will-it-work.

Average income for United States worker 2008, www.census.gov.

U.S. Department of Labor, U.S. Bureau of Labor Statistics, "Consumer expenditures," April 2009.

Visualeconomics.com, "How the average U.S. consumer spends their paycheck." Accessed February 18, 2010, http://www.visualeconomics.com/how-the-average-us-consumer-spends-their-paycheck/.

Tamkins T, "Medical bills prompt more than 60 percent of U.S. bankruptcies." CNN.com, June 5, 2009. Accessed February 18, 2010, http://www.cnn.com/2009/HEALTH/06/05/bankruptcy.medical.bills/.

Arkes HR, Ayton P, "The sunk cost and Concorde effects: Are humans less rational than lower animals?" *Psychological Bulletin* Vol. 125(5), September 1999, pp. 591–600.

Klaczynski P, "Framing effects on adolescent task representations, analytic and heuristic processing, and decision making: Implications for the normative/descriptive gap." *Journal of Applied Developmental Psychology* Vol. 22(3), May-June 2001, pp. 289–309.

Macrae F, "Why keeping up with the Joneses can jeopardize your health." *DailyMail.co.uk, Mail Online*, July 8, 2009. Accessed February 18, 2010, http://www.dailymail.co.uk/health/article-1198236/Why-keeping-Joneses-jeopardise-health.html.

Pew Research Center, "Luxury or necessity? The things we can't live without: the list has grown in the past decade," 2006. Accessed February 18, 2010, http://pewresearch.org/assets/social/pdf/Luxury.pdf.

CHAPTER 4

The Conference Board, "I can't get no . . . job satisfaction, that is. America's unhappy workers." Research Report #1459-09-RR, January 5, 2010.

HRM Guide, "Job Satisfaction." *HRMGuide.com*, February 9, 2008. Accessed February 18, 2010, http://www.hrmguide.com/commitment/job-satisfaction.htm.

Live Science, "Americans hate their jobs more than ever." *MSNBC.com*, February 26, 2007. Accessed February 18, 2010, http://www.msnbc.msn.com/id/17348695/.

Judge TA, et al, "Job Satisfaction as a Reflection of Disposition: A multiple source casual analysis." *Organizational Behavior and Human Decision Processes* Vol. 56(3), December 1993, pp. 388–421.

Arvey RD, et al, "Job satisfaction: environmental and genetic components." *Journal of Applied Psychology* Vol. 74(2), April 1989, pp. 187–192.

Fried Y, et al, "The validity of the job characteristics model: A review and meta-analysis." *Personnel Psychology* Vol. 40(2), 1987, pp. 287–322.

Hackman JR, et al, "Motivation through the design of work: test of a theory." *Organizational Behavior and Human Performance* Vol. 16, 1976, pp. 250–279.

WebMD, "Managing job stress: What causes job stress." April 22, 2009. Accessed February 18, 2010, http://www.webmd.com/balance/stress-management/tc/managing-job-stress-what-causes-job-stress.

Naughton K, "Cyberslacking." *Newsweek,* November 29, 1999. Accessed February 18, 2010, http://www.newsweek.com/id/90366.

Miller K, et al, "Participation, satisfaction, and productivity: A meta-analytic review." *Academy of Management Journal* Vol. 29(4), 1986, pp. 727–753.

The Not for Profit Times, "Busy employees are happier." *The Not for Profit Times,* Vol. 4(9), April 23, 2008.

Foerde K, et al, "Modulation of competing memory systems by distraction." *Proceedings of the National Academy of Sciences* Vol. 103(31), August 1, 2006, pp. 11778–11783.

Rubenstein JS, et al, "Executive control of cognitive processes in task switching." *Journal of Experimental Psychology: Human Perception and Performance* Vol. 27(4), 2001, pp. 763–797.

Gorlick A, "Media multitaskers pay a mental price, Stanford study shows." *Stanford University News*, April 24, 2009. Accessed February 18, 2010, http://news.stanford.edu/news/2009/august24/multitask-research-study-082409.html.

Kanazawa S, Kovar J, "Why beautiful people are more intelligent." *Intelligence* Vol. 32(3), May-June 2004, pp. 227–243.

Lorenz K, "Do pretty people earn more? Research can be at odds over an ugly truth." *CNN.com*, July 11, 2005. Accessed February 18, 2010, http://www.cnn.com/2005/US/Careers/07/08/looks/.

Frieze I, et al, "Attractiveness and income for men and women in management." *Journal of Applied Social Psychology* Vol. 21(13), July 31, 2006, pp. 1039–1057.

Mishra R, "Women's weight found to affect job, income." *The Boston Globe*, May 28, 2005.

The Conference Board, "Obesity costs U.S. companies as much as $45 billion a year, The Conference Board Reports." April 9, 2008. Accessed February 18, 2010, http://www.conference-board.org/UTILITIES/pressDetail.cfm?press_ID=3365.

BNet, "Bosses to workers: Lose the flip-flops-Your life-workplace dress." Accessed February 18, 2010, http://findarticles.com/p/articles/mi_m1272/is_2702_132/ai_110531012/.

Jones D, "Study says flirtatious women get fewer raises, promotions." *USA Today*, August 4,

2005. Accessed February 18, 2010 http://www.usatoday.com/money/workplace/2005-08-04-sex-usat_x.htm.

Vieru T, "Half of all employees bring their work home: This is a major cause of stress." Softpedia.com, January 13, 2010. Accessed February 18, 2010, http://news.softpedia.com/news/Half-of-All-Employees-Bring-Their-Work-Home-131946.shtml.

McGraw M, "Upsetting the balance." *Human Resources Executive Online*, January 26, 2010. Accessed February 18, 2010 http://www.hreonline.com/HRE/story.jsp?storyId=327731007.

Sherk J, "Upwards Leisure Mobility: Americans work less and have more leisure time than ever before." *The Heritage Foundation*, August 31, 2007, Accessed February 18, 2010, http://www.heritage.org/Research/Labor/wm1596.cfm.

Working America, "Bad bosses report 2009." Accessed February 18, 2010, http://www.working america.org/badboss/report.cfm.

Nyberg A, et al, "Managerial leadership and ischaemic heart disease among employees: the Swedish WOLF study." *Occupational and Environmental Medicine* Vol. 66(640), November 27, 2008, pp. 51–55.

Lawson W, "Good boss, bad boss." *Psychology Today*, November 1, 2005. Accessed February 19, 2010, http://www.psychologytoday.com/articles/200510/good-boss-bad-boss.

Gilbreath B, Benson PG, "The contribution of supervisor behaviour to employee psychological well-being." *Work and Stress* Vol 18(3), 2004, pp. 255–266.

The American Management Association, "The high cost of a bad boss." October 2, 2007. Accessed February 19, 2010, http://www.amanet.org/training/articles/The-High-Cost-of-the-Bad-Boss.aspx.

The Street, "How to socialize in the office." MainStreet.com, March 13, 2009. Accessed February 19, 2010 http://www.mainstreet.com/article/career/work/life-balance/how-socialize-office.

RISMedia, "Increase productivity at work by socializing with colleagues." February 14, 2008. Accessed February 19, 2010, http://rismedia.com/2008-02-13/increase-productivity-at-work-by-socializing-with-colleagues/.

Gardner M, "Meet up after work? No thanks, say man U.S. officemates." *The Christian Science Monitor*, March 17, 2008.

Whittell G, "Snakes in suits and how to spot them." *The Times, Times Online*, November 11, 2002. Accessed February 19, 2010, http://www.timesonline.co.uk/tol/life_and_style/article 826475.ece.

Babiak P, Hare R, "Snakes in suits: when psychopaths go to work." Harper Business, May 2006, New York.

Armour S, "Office gossip has never traveled faster, 'thanks' to tech." *USA Today*, September 10, 2007. Accessed February 19, 2010, http://www.usatoday.com/money/workplace/2007-09-09-office-gossip-technology_N.htm.

Randstad USA/Harris Interactive, "Gossip tops biggest workplace pet peeves, according to a Randstad survey." October 29, 2007.

Rosenblum G, "Psst: Men gossip, too, study says." *The Columbus Dispatch*, May 28, 2007. Accessed February 19, 2010, http://www.dispatch.com/live/content/life/stories/2007/05/28/1A_MEN_GOSSIP.ART_ART_05-28-07_D1_R96PJBD.html.

Daily Mail, "Men more likely to gossip than women—survey." *Mail Online*. Accessed February 19, 2010, http://www.dailymail.co.uk/news/article-83255/Men-likely-gossip-women—survey.html.

Campbell L, "Gossip in same-gender and cross-gender friends' conversations." *Personal Relationships* Vol. 2(3), May 20, 2005, pp. 237–246.

Carey B, "Have you heard? Gossip turns out to serve a purpose." *The New York Times*, August 16, 2005.

Black R, "Gossip makes up 80 percent of our conversations—and that might be OK." *The NY Daily News*, September 10, 2009.

Harcourt J, et al, "A national study of middle managers' assessment of organizational communication quality." *Journal of Business Communication* Vol. 28(4), Fall 1991, pp. 348–365.

Tahmincioglu E, "Recession adds fuel to workplace gossip. Job fears, economic woes send the office rumor mill into overdrive." November 30, 2009. Accessed February 19, 2010, http://www.msnbc.msn.com/id/34149723/ns/business-careers/.

Careerbuilder.com, "Forty percent of workers have dated a co-worker, finds annual Career builder.com Valentine's Day survey." February 10, 2009.

Stott P, "Office romance survey 2010." Vault.com. Accessed February 19, 2010.

Society for Human Resource Management/CareerJournal.com, "2006 job retention poll." December 2006.

Gaudin S, "Study: 75% of workers will look for new jobs in 2007." *Information Week Global CIO*, December 20, 2006. Accessed February 19, 2010, http://www.informationweek.com/news/global-cio/training/showArticle.jhtml?articleID=196701147.

CHAPTER 5

Chang VW, et al, "Income disparities in body mass index and obesity in the United States, 1971–2002." *Archives of Internal Medicine* Vol. 165(18), October 10, 2005, pp. 2122–2128.

Carmichael M, "Do we really need a law to protect fat workers?" *The Boston Globe*, August 5, 2007.

Darlin D, "Extra weight, higher costs." *The New York Times*, December 2, 2006. Accessed February 19, 2010, http://www.nytimes.com/2006/12/02/business/02money.html

Liberman N, Shapira O, "Does falling in love make us more creative?" *Scientific American*, September 29, 2009. Accessed February 19, 2010, http://www.scientificamerican.com/article.cfm?id=does-falling-in-love-make.

Sutherland K, "Married men earn a third more than their single counterparts." *The Daily Mail, Mail Online*, January 30, 2010. Accessed February 19, 2010, http://www.dailymail.co.uk/news/article-1247317/Married-men-earn-single-counterparts.html.

Singletary M, "Married college graduates make more money, says Pew report." *The Washington Post*, January 21, 2010. Accessed February 19, 2010, http://www.washingtonpost.com/wp-dyn/content/article/2010/01/20/AR2010012004769.html.

Kaplan RM, et al, "Marital status and longevity in the United States population." *Journal of Epidemiology and Community Health* Vol. 60(9), September 2006, pp. 760–765.

Manzoli L, et al, "Marital status and mortality in the elderly: a systematic review and meta-analysis." *Social Science and Medicine* Vol. 64(1), January 2007, pp. 77–94.

Carroll J, "Most Americans 'very satisfied' with their personal lives." *Gallup*, December 31, 2007. Accessed February 19, 2010, http://www.gallup.com/poll/103483/most-americans-very-satisfied-their-personal-lives.aspx.

Jones JM, "Personal satisfaction ratings decline to lowest levels since 1992." *Gallup*, December 10, 2008. Accessed February 19, 2010, http://www.gallup.com/poll/113050/Personal-Satisfaction-Ratings-Decline-Lowest-Since-1992.aspx.

Index